Cover: Tonopah 1903 (Los Angeles Title Insurance and Trust Co.)

Little Known

Tales In

Nevada

History

By Alton Pryor

Stagecoach Publishing
5360 Campcreek Loop
Roseville, CA. 95747
916-771-8166
stagecoach@surewest.net

3

Little Known

Tales In

Nevada

History

Copyright © 2003 by Alton Pryor

Library of Congress Control Number: 2003098740
ISBN: 0-9747551-0-9

First Printing 2003

Stagecoach Publishing
5360 Campcreek Loop
Roseville, CA. 95747
916-771-8166
stagecoach@surewest.net

*The past is never dead. It's
not even past.* (William Faulkner)

Introduction

Our foray into Nevada's history has been a true joy ride. It was after our good reader reception and success with our several books on California's magnificent history that we decided to venture onward.

Nevada has an abundance of interesting stories from its past. We hope our readers agree with us in our assessment of some of the state's many historic moments.

There are ghost towns and mining camps that have long ceased to exist, but none-the-less worth the visit.

If you can't make the trip in person, we welcome you to travel with us while we explore some of Nevada's interesting pioneers, its vast desert and its curious happenings. Happy to have you along.

Alton Pryor

Table of Contents

9

Chapter 1

Lake Tahoe and its controversies

Sitting like a jewel astride the Nevada-California line, it would seem impossible that something so serene could cause so much conflict. Simply finding a name for the magnificent lake created chaos.

Lake Tahoe, jewel in the Sierra
(Nevada State Highway Department)

Captain John C. Fremont discovered Lake Tahoe, as it is now called, when he was a member of the U.S. Topographical Corps. When he arrived on the scene on February 14, 1844, Fremont first called it Lake Bonpland.

Aimé Jacques Alexandre Bonpland was an eminent French botanist whom Fremont admired, but who had never been to the area, let alone the lake. Fremont's mapmaker, Charles Preuss, however, did not get the word about Fremont's choice. On his charts, he showed the lake as *Mountain Lake.* Fremont

13

apparently later agreed with Preuss and used Mountain Lake on his own reports of 1845-46.

John Bigler, California's third governor had led a rescue party into Lake Valley in the Sierra Nevada to bring out a party of snowbound immigrants. When he returned to *Hangtown,* now Placerville, a group of immigrants proposed the lake be named in his honor. W.M. Eddy, Surveyor General of California, did rename the lake as Lake Bigler to honor him.

This didn't sit that well with those on the eastern side of the Sierra, or even with Californians that were not of the same political persuasion as Governor Bigler.

Bigler was an ardent Democrat and a known supporter of the Southern Cause during the Civil War in 1861. He was also suspected of being involved in the Pacific Confederacy and its shadowy conspiracy to take California out of the Union.

Pro-Union newspaper editors lambasted the "Lake Bigler" name. The Sacramento Union wanted it changed to Sierra Lake, but it was soon pointed out that a Sierra Lake already existed near Downieville Buttes.

The Sacramento Union suggested that the Indian name *Teho* might be appropriate.

The Nevada Transcript of Nevada City was even more adamant than the Union that the name should be changed. "Why the finest sheet of water in the mountains should be named after a fifth rate politician we have never been able to see," the editor seethed.

William Henry Knight, a cartographer, along with Henry DeGroot, a mapmaker, led the revolt against the Lake Bigler name. They began a search for an Indian name. A Captain Jim of the Washoe tribe told DeGroot that *Tah-hoe-ee,* with the accent on the last syllable, meant "big lake" or "water in a high place."

In 1861, Knight gathered data to compile the first map of the Pacific states, and in 1862 the Bancroft Publishing House in San Francisco published this map. Knight deliberately omitted the name Lake Bigler. He urged DeGroot and John S. Hittell to support him in a change of names.

DeGroot claims he induced the U.S. Land Office to change the name officially in 1862. Knight obtained the approval of the Land Office in Washington, D.C., and the new name of "Lake Tahoe" appeared on all subsequent maps and in printed matter from the Department of Interior.

Still another version of the story comes from an article written by Robert G. Dean, of Genoa, Nevada, that was published in the Territorial Enterprise on February 3, 1870.

Dean claimed that he and William VanWagner were owners of the Old Lake House in Lake Valley at the south end of the lake when the Civil War began. As strong Union supporters, they began a search for an Indian name and consulted Captain Jim of the Washoe tribe. Captain Jim told them the name was *Ta-hoo*, meaning "Big Water." Judge Seneca Dean sent this information to the editor of the Sacramento Union, and they got a post office box established at their place with the name *Taho* in December 1863.

There are some that feel calling the body of water Lake Tahoe is a redundancy, technically, as it would mean "Lake Lake."

While the new name was popular in many places, it still had its dissenters. The editor of the San Joaquin *Republican* believed the word had a "vulgar significance."

When the California Legislature was considering naming the lake in 1870, the editor of the Placerville *Mountain Democrat* declared that Tahoe was a renegade Indian who had murdered many whites in pillaging forays on wagon trains, ranches and small settlements.

"Was this therefore a logical choice for the naming of those beautiful waters?" he asked.

The editor of the *State Register* in Carson City agreed with the Mountain Democrat's assessment. Tahoe, the editor said, was an Indian who was disliked even by his own tribe.

A writer for the *Truckee Republican* was even more skeptical. He ventured that the word "Tahoe" was probably the idiomatic Indian word for whiskey, "Big Water."

California's lawmakers, undaunted, with the democrats outnumbering, on February 10, 1870, passed a resolution declaring the lake to be "Bigler" in honor of their fellow party member.

This led Dan DeQuille, a reporter for the *Territorial Enterprise* to quip those lawmakers should now take the next step and make the writing or utterance of the name "Tahoe" a prison offense.

DeQuille also proposed that the Nevada portion of the lake should have a name selected by that state's own lawmakers.

Official road signs at the time, still pointed the traveler to Lake Tahoe, not Lake Bigler. The California Legislature was oblivious to the popularity of the name Tahoe.

It wasn't until July 1945, that lawmakers passed a new statute, declaring, "The Lake known as Bigler shall hereinafter be known as Lake Tahoe."

Resources
1. "This Was Nevada," by Phillip I. Earl
2. Nevada Historical Society
3. "Nevada, The Great Rotten Borough", by Gilman Ostrander.
4. "Historic Spots in California," by Douglas E. Kyle

Chapter 2

Ironic justice in the Comstock

Early in 1850 a Mormon emigrant train headed to California to bastion the stake of the Mormon Church in the western lands. The train camped in the Carson Valley for a number of weeks, waiting for the spring thaw to make the hazardous trek over the Sierra Nevada passable.

While camped there, a number of the party did some prospecting along the Carson River. They found color in the foot of a ravine that cut far up the southern side of Mount Davidson.

With the enthusiasm of newcomers, they named the ravine *Gold Canyon*. When the snows finally melted from the mountain passes, the Mormons recalled their religious commitment, picked up, and headed west for California—leaving behind them what would ultimately lead to be the richest silver strike in American history.

Later, in 1854, the brothers Ethan Allan Grosch and Hosea Ballou Grosch wandered over to Gold Canyon and began prospecting. By the end of 1854, lack of funds forced them to abandon their efforts. It was the same bad luck they had had in California.

The two brothers, perhaps better educated then most prospectors who heeded the call to the gold rush, did suspect there was something more to be had from the ground they had so laboriously worked.

In a letter to their father in early 1856, the brothers wrote, "Ever since our return from Utah we have been trying to get a couple of hundred dollars together for the purpose of making a careful examination of silver lead in Gold Cañon." They were sure it was silver they were seeing in Gold Canyon. It resembled thin sheet-lead.

17

When the brothers returned to Gold Canyon in September of 1856, they confirmed their hopes with the discovery of two silver veins near the head of the canyon. "One of these veins is a perfect monster," they wrote their father. "We have hopes, almost amounting to a certainty, of veins crossing the Cañon at two other points."

Virginia City about 1850

By 1857, the brothers' excitement was justified. "We have followed two shoots down the hill, have a third traced positively, and feel pretty sure there is a fourth. We have pounded up some of each variety of rock and set it to work by the Mexican process.

The rock of the vein looks beautiful, is very soft, and will work remarkably easy. Its colors are violet-blue, indigo-blue, blue-black, and greenish-black."

When assayed, the ore became even more beautiful. It assayed at $3,500 a ton, indicating the brothers may have discovered the great lode itself.

They continued mapping the area and staking claims, supporting themselves meanwhile by prospecting for gold.

Their plan was to outline the silver veins as completely as possible, then return to California for the necessary capital to develop them. Their bad luck then began. First, Hosea pierced his foot with a pick. Gangrene crept in, and by September, he was dead.

Ethan remained long enough to work out the cost of his brother's sickness and burial, and then set out for California to seek money to work the claim. Accompanying him was Richard M. Bucke, a young prospector from Canada.

They were enveloped by an early winter storm at Bigler Lake (now Lake Tahoe) For more than two weeks they wandered lost. They literally crawled into the mining camp with the ironic name of "Last Chance", hungry and nearly frozen. Twelve days later Ethan died. Bucke knew little of the silver discovery made by Ethan and his brother. Suffering an amputated foot, he returned to Canada.

The "monster ledge" that the Grosch brothers identified did begin attracting new prospectors at two points in 1859—at the Ophir claim on the northeastern slopes of Mt. Davidson and at the "Old Red Ledge" about two miles south in Gold Canyon.

It was by historical accident that the ledge of silver-and-gold-bearing ore was named for Henry Comstock, a prospector who had nothing to do with its discovery.

Comstock was often called "Old Pancake", because he subsisted chiefly on flapjacks. He was described as a boastful, loud-voiced, bullying prospector.

Various historians described him as having a superior gift of gall as well as being dimwitted. The lanky, rawboned Henry Paige Comstock was Canadian by birth. As a fur trader and trapper, he had drifted through the west for years when he finally landed at Gold Canyon.

When he arrived at Gold Canyon, he was variously described as indolent, and "little more than half-witted." Still, Comstock possessed the canny ability to be at the right place at the right time.

He brashly moved into the little stone cabin that the Grosch Brothers had previously used, claiming he was doing so by arrangement with the now-dead Ethan Grosch. He claimed the cabin arrangement was granted him in return for keeping claim jumpers away from Ethan's claims.

It was at this time that four prospectors, led by James "Old Virginia" Fennimore, began investigating the area. Besides Fennimore, there was Manny Penrod, Jack Bishop and Joe Winters. Striking early color, the four immediately staked out fifty-foot placer claims.

A few days later, Comstock stumbled upon the scene and took up a fifth claim. The enterprise was soon christened "Gold Hill."

Their gold prospecting was returning eight to twenty-five dollars per man. The trouble was "the damned blue stuff" the prospectors kept encountering as they dug deeper into the earth. Not only was it hard to dig, but it also clogged up their rockers and Long Toms.

As history attests, the "blue stuff" turned out to be far richer than even the gold ore. The quintet of miners had blindly stumbled upon the surface accumulation of the south end of the Comstock Lode. A ten-foot blanket of soil deposited there by the wind and the rains covered it. Gold Hill became the new metropolis of Nevada.

An assault on the Lode was also taking place about a mile over the ridge from Gold Hill at Six-Mile Canyon. Prospectors struck a rich vein of gold there, but just as the miners at Gold Hill had done, they blindly dismissed the "damned blue stuff."

As coincidence, or blind luck would have it, again the mercurial Henry Comstock entered the picture. He had hired Indians to work his Gold Hill claim while he himself began rambling about the hills.

Miners in the Comstock were subjected to extreme temperature changes. The shirtless miners are getting ready to descend into the mine while the clothed miners have just arrived at the surface.

It was in this way he encountered Patrick McLaughlin and Peter O'Riley, the two Irish miners working the Six-Mile Canyon claim. After seeing the rich glint of metal around the edges of the hole they were working, Comstock brazenly informed them they were trespassing.

Comstock lied to the prospectors, saying that months before he had staked out a claim to 160 acres for use as a ranch and that the miners were trespassing. He blustered his way into getting equal shares in the mining operations of the Irishmen. But later he conned them out of even more, telling them the stream they were using to wash their claim was from a spring owned by Comstock and Fennimore. With this assertion, he gained another one hundred feet of claim.

Comstock then rode off to find Fennimore from whom he purchased a share of the spring for a bottle of whiskey and the horse he rode. Comstock now owned claims that bracketed the north and south ends of the Lode, even though at this time he did not realize how valuable the claims he held really were.

James Fennimore, even after being bilked by Comstock, sold out his fifty-foot claim for fifty dollars a foot. All of the other original holders of rich Gold Hill claims did the same.

At the northern, or Ophir end, McLaughlin sold his claim for $3,500 and was ultimately buried at public expense. Penrod held out until the end of 1859, but then sold out for $8,500.

Of the original Ophir owners, only O'Riley refused to sell for any length of time, and even then the $40,000 he did receive was far below his claim's real value. He frittered the money away and ultimately died in an insane asylum.

Even Henry Comstock came up on the short end after all of his lying to gain a foothold on claims worth a fortune. Two months after the lode was discovered for the riches it contained, Comstock sold off his claims for only $11,000, at the same time congratulating himself for having pulled the wool over the eyes of "another greedy Californian".

After failed attempts to recapture his moment of glory at other sites, Comstock finally killed himself in Bozeman, Montana.

Resources

1. "Gold and Silver in the West," by T.H. Watkins
2. "Comstock Mining and Miners," by Eliot Lord, geologist
3. "The Silver State," by James W. Hulse
4. "The Story of the Mine", by Charles H. Shinn
5. "The Big Bonanza," by C.B. Glasscock
6. "History of Nevada," By Russell R. Elliott

An excerpt from "The Big Bonanza" by Dan DeQuille, a reporter with the Territorial Enterprise

"About three fourths of the prospecting miners who came over from California packed their traps on the backs of donkeys, and, driving these before them, boldly, if not swiftly, scaled the Sierras. These donkeys became a great nuisance about the several camps.

"All became thieves of the most accomplished type. They would steal flour, sugar, bacon, beans, and everything eatable about the camp. They would even devour gunnysacks in which bacon had been packed, old woolen shirts, and almost everything else but the picks and shovels.

"The donkeys would be seen demurely grazing on the flats and on the hillsides when the miners left camp in the morning to go out prospecting, but all the time had one eye upon every movement that was made. Hardly were the miners out of sight ere the donkeys were in camp, with heads in the tents devouring all within reach.

"When the miners returned, the donkeys were all out picking about on the hillsides as calmly as though nothing had happened; but the swearing in camp as the work of the cunning beasts came to light would have furnished any ordinary bull-drive a stock of oaths that he could not exhaust in six months.

"One of these donkeys—too confiding—was caught in the act. Many of the miners used a kind of flour called 'self-rising.' There was mixed with it when it was ground all of the ingredients used in the manufacture of yeast powders. All the miner had to do in making bread from this flour was to add the proper quantity of water and mix it, when it 'came up' beautifully.

"The donkey in question had struck a sack of this flour and had eaten all he could hold of it. He went to the spring near the camp and drank a quantity of water. When we came home that evening Mr. Donkey was still at the spring. The self-rising principle in the flour had done its work. The beast was as round as an apple and his legs stood out like those of a carpenter's bench. He was very dead. Here was one of the thieves. Cunning as he had been, he was caught at least, and with 'wool in his teeth.'"

Chapter 3

He let the big one get away

Shorty Harris always seemed to come out on the wrong end of the stick, no matter what the deal. The gold claims that he kept always turned out shallow. Those that he sold made the buyer rich.

As seemed true with each of his endeavors, Shorty was consistently late at arriving at newfound gold strikes. He arrived late in Tonopah and Goldfield and the myriad other spots such as the Keane Wonder where he hoped to stake his claim.

In the summer of 1904, Shorty decided to return to an area where he had tried prospecting before. E.I Cross was at the Keane Wonder when Shorty made his decision.

"Shorty," I'd like to go with you," said Cross.

"Your chance is good," Shorty replied. "Come along."

The pair packed their four burros and headed out, along with some other prospectors who had joined the Keane Wonder rush and met with disappointment.

As Shorty started breaking the quartz on the hill they were prospecting, he was soon dazzled with the sight of free gold.

"The quartz was just full of free gold, and it was the original genuine green bullfrog rock. Talk about rich rock! Why, gee whiz, it was great. We took the stuff back to the spring and panned it, and we certainly went straight up. The very first boulder was as rich in gold as anything I had ever seen," Shorty said later.

When they ground up some of the rock, it panned out rich in gold. Harris seized upon the idea that this one could be the big one, and one claim he would hold onto.

Miners' Union parades down Golden Street in Rhyolite in 1906.

There was scarcely a white man within fifty miles of this spot. Old Man Beatty did have a little ranch in the area, but he was now deceased. As far as Shorty knew, there was only one other white family between Manse and Thorp's Wells—a distance of about 100 miles.

The two men checked the area closely and staked out what they considered would be the best claims. They also staked out a mill site and filed a claim for water rights. They then loaded up all the samples they could and headed for Goldfield.

On the way, they stopped at Beatty's Ranch, and word of the strike took on lightening speed. The word spread so fast that one newspaper reporter claimed the two men met prospectors coming at them from Goldfield when they were still ten miles out and that when the two discoverers reached Goldfield, all of Goldfield was staking claims near the Bullfrog.

Bullfrog mining camp drew many prospectors, both men and women, with a wish to get rich.   (Nevada Historical Society)

Shorty's credit was good at every bar in Goldfield, and he exercised the privilege at every one of them. After six days of drinking, the drunken Shorty signed a deed to the Bullfrog for $1000, a circumstance he could not later recall.

"And let me tell you," Shorty predicted, "the Bullfrog District is going to be the banner camp of Nevada after all. I have said so from the beginning and I still say it. I'm no tenderfoot at the prospecting business. If they will put money into the ground here—sink on these mineral showings—like Rube Bryan has in the Pioneer, there will be all kinds of mines in the Bullfrog District."

A Bullfrog mines certificate issued
during the heyday of the Bullfrog Gold District.

The diminutive Shorty prospected for gold in the Death Valley country for another 25 years or so. He died in Big Pine, California, in 1934. On a bronze plaque, which Shorty himself composed, is his epitaph: "Here lies Shorty Harris, a single blanket jackass prospector."

Resources

1. "Helldorados, Ghosts and Camps", by Norman D. Weis.
2. "Rhyolite, Death Valley's Ghost City of Golden Dreams
3. "Death Valley and the Amargosa," by Richard E. Lingenfelter.
4. "History of Nevada," by Russell R. Elliott
4. "Ghost Towns of Nevada," by Donald C. Miller

Chapter 4

Nevada history dates to stone age

The history of man in Nevada dates back as much as 10,000 to 12,000 years. But even before the time that man roamed the deserts, about 20 to 30 thousand years ago, the territory of Nevada and most of the west was going though the end of the great Ice Age.

Scientists from the Nevada universities at both Las Vegas and Reno have found evidence of Paleolithic (Stone Age) humans at Tule Springs in the Sheep Range about 15 miles from Las Vegas. Scientists identified eleven bone tools they believed humans used between 12,000 and 13,000 years ago.

The higher mountains of Nevada were once covered with ice, and many of the higher valleys were filled with glaciers. The lower basins were filled with great lakes, which were frozen in the winter.

Each summer the ice on the mountains would melt, keeping the lakes in the basins full. All of this water kept the area that is now desert covered in lush vegetation.

Little is known about who the first Nevadans were, but historians seem to agree it was the Anasazi, which means "ancient ones." No bones have been found to support their existence, but their artwork associated with the vanished animals of the past is left to tell the tale.

Near the Carson Sink, in Tonopah, Beatty, and in Washoe Valley, rock hunters have found "Clovis points" made an estimated 10,000 years ago. These are stone dart points, apparently used as hunting instruments long before the invention of the bow and arrow.

Petroglyhs found in Condor Canyon southeast of Pioche.

Dart points have also been found near Winnemucca Lake and near the Humboldt Sink in northwestern Nevada. Scientists uncovered hand woven baskets that rested in caves for 5,700 years.

The first written report of archeological remains in Nevada came in 1827 in a letter from the fur trader and mountain man Jedediah Smith to William Clark, superintendent of Indian Affairs. The letter informed Clark of Smith's discovery of a flint knife and pipe in a salt cave in a mountain near the Virgin River.

Early humans searched out caves and rock shelters for safety. They stored their food supplies and other precious objects there, and often died there. Many sites of this kind exist in Nevada. The region was a once quite wet area, with vast lakes and big inland rivers that gradually became dry under conditions that preserved human artifacts.

Scientists feel they have confirmed that the people who lived in the Lovelock Cave near Lake Lahontan 3,000 years ago knew nothing about the bow and arrow; they relied upon the dart as their main weapon for killing game.

Archeologists found many well-preserved tools as well as rabbit skins and feathers fashioned into clothing in the cave. They also found decoy ducks made of tule reeds, which were painted with appropriate colors for attracting other birds.

It isn't clear what happened to the Lovelock Cave people when the waters at Lake Lahontan receded. These people knew nothing of agriculture. Did they adapt to conditions, accept migrating groups from elsewhere, and become ancestors of the modern Northern Paiutes?

One of the most controversial sites showing early man in Nevada is Gypsum Cave, located about twenty miles east of Las Vegas in a limestone spur of the Frenchman Mountains.

Here, great beds of ground sloth dung, in which were imbedded bones, horny claws, and the hair of the sloth, were revealed in excavations made in 1930 and 1931.

The picture above shows a reconstruction of Jefferson's ground sloth from the University of Iowa Museum of Natural History.

Some scientists believe that early man, called the Anasazi, or *Ancient Ones,* lived in Nevada ten to twenty thousand years ago, or 8,000 to 18,000 B.C.

Following this period, the summers and the winters continued to get warmer, the Great Basin dried up; the Mammoth, the Mastodon, and the ground sloth disappeared.

After the Anasazi came the generation commonly referred to as the "Basket Makers." These people knew little of agriculture or pottery making.

Little more was changed, other than adopting the bow and arrow, until the first white men arrived. They lived in dugouts or pit dwellings (circular huts partly sunken in the ground).

Eventually, Pueblo Indians from northern Arizona ventured into the Moapa Valley region, introducing cultivation of cotton, beans and squashes, along with improved methods of building houses.

It is unknown if the Pueblo were conquerors or came in peacefully. The end result, however, was the creation of the *Pueblo Grande de Nevada* or what is commonly referred to as the Lost City.

Something apparently drove the people away from the Lost City. It isn't known if it was the many years of dry seasons, years of floods, or wild nomadic tribes that drove them away. Pueblo settlements were later located high atop mesas to provide for better protections from floods.

Pre-historic findings are all around Nevada. Archeologists in 1930 discovered the claws, hair and skull of an ancient beast, the ground sloth, a huge bear-like herbivorous animal that had been there as much as 10,000 years ago.

At its peak, the Lost City stretched out for four or five miles, and as much as a mile wide. It included farmlands, outlying small dwellings and villages scattered throughout the valley.

Resources
1. "The Silver State," by James W. Hulse
2. . "History of Nevada," by Russell R. Elliott

Chapter 5

Beatty named postmaster but could neither read nor write

When Montellion Murray Beatty wandered in from the desert, he carried all his worldly goods packed on two burros.

Beatty was taken in by Paiute Indians who figured he would remain with them only a couple of days to rest and then would head out again. As day after day went by, there was no indication that Beatty was going to leave.

The situation dragged on for some weeks. Eventually, the Indians held a meeting to discuss their paleface guest. It was decided he should be asked to leave. The leader of the group

Montellion Murray Beatty
(Nevada Historical Society)

gave Beatty their stern decision, but he continued to hang on.

Finally, the Indians decided they would take an even more permanent means of getting the guest to leave. It was agreed that they would kill him.

It was then that the chief's daughter, *Mahanagos*, stepped forward to defend him. Mahanagos, which means *spring of the desert*, apparently was the reason all along that Beatty delayed his departure.

At night, after Beatty had wrapped himself in his blankets and gone to sleep under the desert stars, the Paiutes held a second conference. Beatty, they decided, would be dispatched without further ado.

Again, Mahanagos interceded. It was agreed then that Beatty's life would be spared, but only if he would be willing to marry Mahanagos. Beatty was willing, and a wedding took place a few days later with all the ceremony the Indians could muster.

Beatty abandoned his dreams of someday striking a rich lode of silver or gold. Instead, he settled in with his bride and became, for all intents and purposes, an Indian. He settled in the Oasis Valley with the Mahanagos, and raised a number of children in their remote part of the desert.

Beatty was described as a generous, hardworking family man who made his ranch a welcome home to all who passed his way. He lived a quiet life until the discovery of the Bullfrog mines.

In 1904, when gold was indeed found at nearby Bullfrog and Rhyolite, the Amargosa area was swept along in the excitement that hits any gold rush town. This is what caused the towns of Rhyolite and Bullfrog to first come into being.

Bitten again by the gold bug, Beatty sold his ranch for $10,000, after giving his name to the town, and started a new ranch at Cow Creek over in Death Valley.

Three railroads soon reached the town that was named after Beatty. By the fall of 1907; the Las Vegas & Tonopah, the Bullfrog & Goldfield and the Tonopah & Tidewater had all started making stops there. Homes, businesses, schools, churches, hotels and theatres soon graced the once wide-open spaces.

This photo shows the Beatty family on their ranch. The photo was taken about 1900. (Nevada Historical Society)

Montellion Beatty prospered since many of the establishments were located on his land. When a post office was established January 19, 1905, Beatty became the postmaster, even though he could neither read nor write.

He left these details to his assistant, R.A. Gibson. Beatty dedicated himself to boosting his town's future, which was often touted as "The Chicago of Nevada."

On December 13, 1908, Montellion Beatty fell from a wagon and fractured his skull. He died the following day without regaining consciousness.

While the Bullfrog gold district declined, the town of Beatty became a quiet roadside community at the junction of Highway 95 and State Route 58.

Beatty now calls itself the "Gateway to Death Valley". It is located six miles from the Nevada-California border, 120 miles north of Las Vegas and 330 miles south of Reno. Three peaks, Bare Mountain, Sawtooth Mountain, and the Bullfrog Hills surround the town.

35

Beatty has a population of about 1,800 people and is situated in Nye County.

Resources

1. "This Was Nevada" by Phillip I. Earl
2. Nevada Historical Society
3. "Death Valley & the Amargosa," by Richard E. Lingenfelter
4. Beatty Chamber of Commerce

Chapter 6

Nevada's last lynching

Monday, March 5, 2001 wasn't a day that was widely celebrated, or even mentioned, but it was a somewhat significant day in Nevada history. It was the 96th anniversary of the State's last lynching.

The hanging occurred in Hazen, Nevada, a railroad siding located 40 miles east of Reno.

The hanging victim was William "Red" Wood, described by the Reno Evening *Gazette* as a "notorious thug and all around bad man."

The body of William "Nevada Red" Wood, hangs from a telegraph pole in Hazen, Nevada.

(Nevada Historical Society)

Wood was a morphine addict and a saloon owner. His crime was the supposed killing of his partner and saloon co-owner. Woods was caught in the act of robbery outside the Hazen depot the night before.

The town of Hazen attracted a lot of rough and undesirable characters. Canal laborers on the Newlands Project were often assaulted and robbed in the streets and alleys. Churchill County officials assigned only one man with the job of keeping the peace. That man was Judd Allen, a local hotelkeeper.

Red Wood was an ex-convict and served time at Sing Sing Prison in New York, and in the Iowa State Penitentiary. He had been associated with Jerry McCarthy in a saloon operation at Derby, another canal camp.

When McCarthy died under mysterious circumstances in January 1904, "Red" Wood left Derby and headed for Reno. He was arrested a year later for trying to rob a man outside a Commercial Row saloon. He was released when his intended victim refused to testify.

Wood then showed up in Hazen, where he and a friend tried to waylay and rob two canal laborers near the railroad depot. The robbery attempt was thwarted when the station agent and a telegraph operator intervened.

Woods stopped when the telegraph operator fired a shotgun over his head. He was handed over to Constable Allen, who placed him under arrest. Woods was incarcerated in the town's temporary wooden jail.

About 2 a.m., a mob assembled and marched to the jail. They unceremoniously opened the jail door with an ax and ordered Wood to come out.

"For God's sake, no!" Woods pleaded. "I'm innocent, spare my life."

Wood was pulled from his cell and dragged to a telegraph pole thirty feet away. One end of a rope was tied to the base of the pole and the other end was thrown over the pole's crossbar. The noose at its other end was placed around Wood's neck.

A woman having breakfast in Constable Allen's hotel the next morning first saw the body hanging limply from the pole. She thought it was a cruel joke and that the body hanging from the rope was simply a dummy.

The body was given an immediate burial and citizens in Hazen refused to talk to Reno newsmen. Sheriff Robert Shirley of Fallon, Nevada, refused to become involved. Governor John Sparks said he too preferred to leave the matter to county officials.

One enterprising man from Hazen did a brisk business by cutting up the rope used to hang Wood and selling the pieces as souvenirs. One story adds that when the entrepreneur finished selling all of the rope pieces, there were still others who wanted to buy souvenirs. So he got another rope and cut it up.

The Reno Evening Gazette described the lynching in some detail:

38

The mob worked quietly and it was not until the sun lighted up the country that the people of this place discovered the stiffened body swinging at the end of a rope in the heart of the city.

The story ran on the front page next to reports on the divorce trial of Col. W.F. "Buffalo Bill" Cody in North Platte, Nebraska, and his wife's denials that she ever tried to poison him.

Vigilante justice came to an end in Nevada with the hanging of Wood. It was the end of a tradition that began in 1858 with the lynching of "Lucky Bill" Thorrington in Carson Valley. According to one report, Thorrington (or Thorington), a Mormon, was hanged because of practicing polygamy. The locals strongly disapproved of the practice.

Lynchings in the old West were different than those of the South, where Ku Klux Klan racists killed innocent blacks. In the west, most victims of lynch law were white—suspected killers, highway robbers and cattle rustlers. Some historians say the number of vigilante lynchings was exaggerated.

There were some reports that by the time photographers arrived from Reno, Wood's body had already been buried on the outskirts of town. Always willing to please, the locals dug up the body and strung him up on the pole again to help send a message to villains to stay clear of Hazen.

Resources

1. "This Was Nevada," by Phillip I. Earl, Nevada Historical Society.
2. Las Vegas Review Journal
3. Reno Evening Gazette

Rules for Teachers

1.   Teachers each day fill lamps, clean chimney.

2.   Each teacher will bring a bucket of water and a scuttle of coal for the day's session.

3.   Make your pens carefully. You may whittle nibs to the individual taste of the pupils.

4.   Men teachers may take one evening each week for courting purposes, or two evenings a week if they go to church regularly.

5.   After ten hours in school, the teachers may spend the remaining time reading the Bible or other good books.

6.   Women teachers who marry or engage in unseemly conduct will be dismissed.

7.   Every teacher should lay aside from each pay a goodly sum of his earnings for the benefit during his declining years so that he will not become a burden on society.

8.   Any teacher who smokes, uses liquor in any form, frequents pool or public halls, or get shaved in a barber shop will give good reason to suspect his worth, intention, integrity and honesty.

9.   The teacher, who performs his labor faithfully and without fault for five years, will be given an increase of twenty-five cents per week in his pay, providing the Board of Education approves.

(Sparks Heritage Museum)

Chapter 7

Tybo averts white vs. Asian war

An Indian, whose name has been forgotten, found ore in 1865. White men quickly scented the rich discovery and the town of Tybo, Nevada was born. The ore produced there was silver, lead and zinc.

The Belmont *Courier*, on August 1, 1874, *screamed* the news that the ore from the Slavonian Chief mine had assayed at a rate of $20,786.01 per ton. The newspaper again reported in May 1875, that ore from a ledge varying from 12 to 16 inches in thickness had assayed at $3,000 per ton.

Tybo is located on the eastern slope of the Hot Creek Range about eighty miles south of Eureka, Nevada.

The scarcity of labor in the area very nearly brought about a war between white and Chinese laborers.

Mines and mills were, from the beginning, staffed largely with Central Europeans and Cornish and Irish emigrants, who ironically, used to fight among themselves.

The shortage of workers became critical and labor contractors for the Two G Mining Company brought in Chinese coolies to cut wood to fire the charcoal kilns. The importing of such labor was in violation of an agreement the miners had with the owners to use only white labor at the mines.

Mine owners countered that it had been unable to procure white workmen in sufficient numbers and were forced to accept whatever workers were available. The mineworkers that had been prone to battle among themselves, now banded together.

Tybo post office and general store in the 1870s.

As miners were wont to do, they collected in the saloons and on street corners. Their discussions led to a mass meeting. The miners openly declared a lust for blood—Chinese blood. The miners bolstered their courage with vast amounts of liquor and descended on the sleeping charcoal camp of the Chinese.

Cracking bullwhips, shooting their pistols in the air, and shouting drunken curses, the miners were able to send the terrified Chinese fleeing to the surrounding hillsides.

When morning came, there were no woodcutters to supply fuel for the charcoal kilns. The charcoal contractors began scouting the nearby hills in search of the scattered Chinese woodcutters.

They gathered them from their many hiding places, and, like a herd of sheep, drove them back to their woodcutting and stoking duties. They were ordered to resume work while watchmen stood over them with loaded Winchesters.

When nightfall descended, the white labors again rose up. Under the influence of the plentiful raw liquor dispensed in the downtown taverns, 200 angry miners, armed with guns, descended on the area with the aim of cleaning out the Chinese.

Since armed guards still stood at their stations, overseeing the Chinese workmen, the enthusiasm of the miners dimmed, but they did issue an ultimatum. The miners gave the contractors 24 hours to get rid of the Chinese workmen.

When the 24-hour grace period ended, and the Chinese were still working, a second ultimatum was issued: Either the Chinese leave camp before nightfall or both they and their employers would be ridden out of town on rails.

The white laborers were thoroughly aroused and bloodshed seemed inevitable. The Chinese had no desire to continue participating in what could lead to all-out war, and offered to leave the district in exchange for the fare to Eureka.

The Anti-Asiatic League readily provided stage fares to avert an altercation that might have taxed Tybo's tiny cemetery,

Located eight miles off U.S. Highway 6 in central Nye County, Tybo was as lively a mining camp as any in the state in the 1870s. Like many Nevada camps, Tybo has its share of lost treasure stories.

The citizens of Tybo were distrustful of banks. They were more inclined to bury their money than entrust it to institutions that could be robbed any day of the week. How many of these caches were lost or forgotten is not known with any certainty, but surely something is still out there.

One lost treasure story concerns a gambler who happened into town on a payday weekend in 1876 and picked up some $3,000 in gold coins in a marathon poker game. There was talk around town that he had used a marked deck and several men were said to be planning to waylay him when he departed.

The rumor got back to him and he had the driver of the Belmont stage stop in Kiln Canyon, just out of town. Walking out through the sagebrush with his money in a canvas sack, he returned empty-handed a few minutes later, telling the driver that he would be back when he thought it was safe. Three days later, he was shot and killed in a Belmont saloon.

There is also the story of the Portuguese charcoal contractor who followed the tradition of burying his profits rather than banking them. He did well in the charcoal business, hiring Chinese laborers to cut pinion and juniper and operate his kilns.

In June 1877, he did not return from Tybo where he had gone to hire more laborers. When his men investigated, they found him on the ground next to the road into town, dead of a broken neck, having apparently been thrown by his horse.

He had no local relatives and several parties of men came out to the kilns in subsequent weeks to look into his supposed fortune. The woodcutters said that The Portuguese contractor would ride out to the northwest every few days and be gone less than an hour. They suspected that some $5,000 in gold coinage was buried out there somewhere, but later searches turned up nothing.

The name Tybo is believed to be from the Shoshone word, *Tybbabo*, which means, "white man's district."

Resources

1. "Ghosts of the Glory Trail", By Nell Marbarger
2. Dave Bethke website:
   http://home.houston.rr.com/bethland/tybo.html
3. Phillip I. Earl, Curator of History for Nevada Historical Society
4. "Ghost Towns of Nevada," by Donald C. Miller.

Chapter 8

The Verdi train Robbery

Nothing created more excitement for Nevada citizens than the November 4, 1870, train robbery near Verdi, located about 10 miles west of Reno. It was the second train robbery ever in the United States and the first on the Pacific Slope.

The robbery gave Nevada the dubious honor of being one of the first states with a set of outlaws daring enough to stop and rob an express train. The first train robbery in the United States occurred when the Reno Brothers gang held up a train near Seymour, Indiana, shortly after the close of the Civil War.

The Verdi robbery involved John T. Chapman, a former Sunday school teacher, who for some reason decided that stealing was a better and quicker way to get money than was hard labor.

Chapman's original intention was to rob a Wells Fargo stagecoach. His ambition was frustrated by the fact that Wells Fargo, after heavy losses from highwaymen, had instituted a new policy of having armed guards on all its stagecoach shipments, as well as guards riding on horseback behind the coaches.

Chapman then hooked up with noted stagecoach robbers Big Jack Davis and John Squires. Others in the group were Tilton Cockerill, James Gilchrist, and R.A. "Sol" Jones. Except for Chapman and Jones, all were hard and toughened outlaws, experienced in stagecoach holdups.

John E. Chapman, center, was a former Sunday school teacher, who collaborated with Tilton Cockerill, James Gilchrist, and R.A. "Sol" Jones. (Nevada Historical Society)

Jack Davis and John Squires joined in the robbery.
(Nevada Historical Society)

Rather than tackle Wells Fargo's armed guards on its stagecoaches, the group decided they would rob Central Pacific's Overland Express No. 1 train. They selected Big Jack Davis, as their leader.

Davis was a well-known Virginia City gambler, but had become proficient at robbing stagecoaches, as well. His success was so good, in fact, that Davis opened his own processing mill to rework the stolen bullion he gathered in his holdups.

The gang decided the isolated town of Verdi would be the ideal spot to stop the Central Pacific's proud Overland Express No. 1 as it headed down the east slope of the Sierra toward Reno. Under Big Jack's direction, the gang carefully plotted their strategy.

Chapman was dispatched to San Francisco to get information on the train's schedule and its valuable cargo. The train, he learned, was carrying $41,800 in gold pieces and $8,800 in silver bars. It was headed for Virginia City, the payroll for the rich Yellow Jacket Mine at Gold Hill. Chapman telegraphed this information to Sol Jones, who relayed it to the other gang members.

The robbery was almost thwarted because express train No. 1 was delayed at a siding in Cisco, California because of an accident to a westbound freight. This caused a great deal of uneasiness to the five men pacing the platform at the Verdi station.

As the express train slowed, but pulled away from the Verdi station without stopping, the five gang members, all wearing masks, swung aboard.

Two of them climbed into the cab of the engine and covered the engineer and fireman with six-shooters. The engineers surrendered the engine to the hold-up men at once.

Another gang member boarded the front platform of the express car, while two others took command of the rear platform.

The train proceeded about half a mile east of Verdi, and the robbers ordered the engineer to whistle "down brakes." *(This was*

47

before the days of air brakes and one short blast of the whistle brought brakemen to the platforms to set the brakes)

The down brakes whistle was also a signal to the three men on the express car to cut the bell rope and pull the coupling pin at the rear of the car. The engineer was then ordered to "Give Her Steam."

About six miles east of Verdi, the locomotive was brought to a halt. The rest of the train was left behind, standing on a downgrade. A knock on the door of the express car surprised Frank Minch, the express messenger.

Minch asked, "Who's there?" The reply was, "Marshall." Expecting to see Conductor Marshall, the messenger unlocked the sliding door. Instead of facing Conductor Marshall, Minch found himself confronted by the muzzle of a double-barreled shotgun. He surrendered without a fight.

The outlaws, after locking the trainmen and messenger inside the mail compartment, broke the strongbox open with a pick. They then threw the Wells Fargo sacks through the side door of the car and into the brush. They left the train, shouldered their booty, and disappeared into the darkness.

At 8 o'clock the next morning, Sheriff Charley Pegg received a message from the Wells Fargo agent at Virginia City that read: "Train robbed between Truckee and Verdi; robbers gone south."

A Washoe County officer went to the scene of the robbery, where he discovered a footprint quite different from the others. A boot with a small heel made the unusual track. Dudes or gamblers generally wore such boots.

A hunting party, arriving at the Sardine Valley House at Sardine Valley, California, was told that three strangers had lodged there the night before.

Two had left early in the morning and the other one was still in his room. When James Burke and his party arrived, bandit James Gilchrist mistook the hunting party for sheriff's deputies. He dashed out the back door and hid in the privy.

Burke found the man and decided to make a citizen's arrest. Burke and his men found six $20 gold pieces that were apparently part of the train robbery.

Washoe County Under-sheriff James Kinkead also had tracked the fleeing train robbers to the Sardine Valley House. With Gilchrist already under arrest, the landlady described in detail the description of the two men that had left earlier.

She said that one of the men was heading toward Sierra Valley in California, where his brother, Joe, lived. Kinkead arrived in Loyalton in Sierra Valley about midnight.

He roused the landlord of the only hotel, and asked if there were any strange guests in the house. The landlord replied he had one, but his description didn't fit either of the two men sought by the lawman. Kinkead decided he would check out the guest anyway.

The landlord gave him a candle and directed Officer Kinkead to room 14. The hotel had just been built and not yet painted. Because of the damp weather, the door on room 14 would not shut tight enough to lock.

The roomer inside had simply placed a chair under the knob inside and gone to bed, feeling he was secure against intruders.

When Kinkead arrived at room 14, he gently pushed the door until the chair moved enough so the officer could get his arm through the crack and quietly remove the obstruction.

The first thing he noticed on entering the room was the small heel of a boot lying on the floor, identical to one at the scene of the robbery. The occupant was still sleeping soundly.

He didn't awaken even when Kinkead removed a six-shooter from under his pillow. Kinkead found enough evidence in the room to convict the train robbers.

The entire gang was rounded up in less than four days after the robbery occurred. Forty thousand dollars of the loot was recovered.

(Author's note: Guy Rocha, Nevada State Archivist, says to be historically correct, the train robbery was not at Verdi,

Nevada, but at a place called "Hunter's Crossing," a Truckee River crossing on the emigrant trail. It had a post office from 1867 to 1870 and was a connecting point to an area from Virginia City and the Comstock Mines)

Resources

1. "This Was Nevada," by Phillip I. Earl
2. Nevada Historical Society
3. Report of James H. Kinkead
4. Central Pacific Railroad History Museum website: http://cprr.org/Museum/Robbery.html

Chapter 9

Battle at Pyramid Lake

Pyramid Lake was formerly Lake Lahonton, Nevada's largest and most famous of its prehistoric lakes.   (Reno New Service.)

Thirty-five miles northeast of Reno there is a lake that is approximately 15 miles long and 11 miles wide, and covers 112,000 square miles. The lake measures 350 deep at its deepest point.

The serenity and peacefulness of what is called America's most beautiful desert lake belies the battle that occurred at that site May 12, 1860 between Paiute Indians and white settlers.

From most accounts, it was three white men that initiated the battle when they kidnapped two Indian women at Williams

Station. A band of rescuing Indians subsequently killed the three white men and burned Williams Station.

When news of the killings reached the Indian Council at Pyramid Lake, Numaga, the Indian leader of the Pyramid Lake Paiute tribe, is reported to have said, "There is no longer any use for counsel; we must prepare for war, for the soldiers will now come here to fight us."

As Numaga, called "Young Winnemucca" by the whites, had predicted, a volunteer army of white settlers and miners gathered detachments from Genoa, Carson City, Silver City, and Virginia City.

There were 105 volunteers in all. They were poorly armed, badly mounted, and almost wholly unorganized. Even so, most of the men felt there would not be much of a fight. Some expected it to be a rather good time, where they might kill a few Indians and capture several ponies.

When the volunteer army, led by Major William Ormsby, arrived at Williams Station, they found and buried the bodies of the three men killed by the Indians, and elected to proceed on to Pyramid Lake.

But the Indians were ready.

The volunteers had proceeded a short distance beyond the present location of Nixon, Nevada, when they sighted a line of horse-mounted Indians. They were just out of gunshot range, and on an elevated stretch of land to the army's right front line.

It appeared that the Indians numbered about the same as the volunteer white army, increasing the confidence of the volunteers.

An order was given to dismount and tighten saddle girths. One volunteer, with a globe-sighted rifle, fired at the Indians, but without effect.

Again mounted, a detachment of thirty men charged toward the Indians while the remainder of the army proceeded at a slower pace. When the army reached the higher ground, they were surprised to find the Indians had mysteriously disappeared, even though the terrain offered little opportunity for concealment.

To the army's surprise, another line of mounted warriors appeared, these too, keeping just beyond rifle range. The Indians formed a semicircle which extended dangerously far to the south.

As the whites pondered whether they had charged into a trap, the fighting began.

Indians materialized from behind sagebrush on both sides of the volunteer detachment, and began pouring a hail of bullets and arrows into the whites. Essentially, within the next few minutes, the battle was lost.

The white volunteers realized they had entered a clever trap. In an attempt to escape, the whites turned toward the west, seeking shelter among the cottonwood trees lining the riverbank.

The Indian attack, however, had been well planned, and two bands of mounted warriors emerged from the trees and charged toward the whites.

Some accounts say that the Indian Chief Numaga made his last attempt to prevent tragedy. He spurred his horse between the charging Indians and the whites, and attempted a parley. But in the confusion, the Indians swept past him, killing untold numbers of the volunteer army.

In the melee, Major Ormsby was shot in the mouth and both arms, and was overtaken and killed. Some of the white volunteer army reached the site of what is now Wadsworth, and were able to escape.

The number of white casualties has never been definitely determined. It is probable that many wounded men died between Pyramid Lake and Virginia City. One summary of estimates indicates that at least seventy men remained unaccounted for.

Fear of an Indian attack spread. In Virginia City, women and children were barricaded in an unfinished stone building. At Silver City, in a stone fort overlooking Devil's Gate, a wooden cannon with iron hoops was constructed and filled with scrap iron.

It was fortunate that the expected Indian attacked did not occur, for when the cannon was fired at a later date, it exploded and showered shrapnel in all directions.

No further contact with the Indians was made and the volunteers were disbanded on June 7, 1860.

Eventually, Colonel Frederick W. Lander negotiated a peace treaty with the Paiutes. He met with Numaga at a hot springs on the emigrant road. History records that this meeting between Numaga and Colonel Lander was the beginning of peace between the white man and the main body of the Northern Paiute of Pyramid.

President U.S. Grant issued the following executive order on March 23, 1874:

The President
March 23, 1874
Executive Mansion

> *It is hereby ordered that the tract of country known and occupied as the Pyramid Lake Indian Reservation in Nevada, as surveyed by Eugene Moore, in January, 1865, and indicated by red lines, according to courses and distances given in tabular form on accompanying diagrams, but withdrawn from sale or other disposition, and set apart for the Pah-Ute and other Indians residing thereon.*
> *(signed) U.S. Grant*

The Pyramid Lake reservation today is locked in a three-way struggle with ranching and farming interests and the rapidly growing municipalities of Reno and Sparks.

All three entities are dependent on water from the Truckee River that flows from Lake Tahoe in the Sierra range and empties finally into Pyramid Lake. Before it gets there, it flows through the metropolitan centers and undergoes diversion to downstream agricultural land.

The Pyramid Lake Indians are claiming water rights under old treaties, protesting that the level of the prehistoric lake is dropping each year and that the fisheries are being endangered.

Resources

1. "The Desert Lake," by Sessions S. Wheeler
2. "The Silver State," by James W. Hulse
3. "This Was Nevada," Phillip I. Earl
4. "With Curry's Compliments," by Doris Cerveri
5. "History of Nevada," by Russell B. Elliott

Chapter 10

Carson City: *"One man's dream"*

In the spring of 1858, Abraham Curry, accompanied by a few friends, drifted across the windswept area known as Eagle Valley looking for any opportunity that might befit a man of his foresight.

Curry was no dawdler. He was eager to get things done. Leaving his friends to set up camp, Curry galloped the few miles to Genoa, looking for a suitable site on which to build a general merchandizing store.

He found a lot that he liked, but was unable to get the owner to come down in price. Curry refused to pay the $1,000 asking price. The nettled Curry rode off in a huff, declaring that Genoa could do without him. He would build his own town.

In 1851, ranchers had settled in Eagle Valley. It is said

Abraham Curry

that a group of well-connected attorneys, whose names now adorn street signs, bought the richest part of the valley for $500 and a remuda of horses. Abe Curry was a junior partner in the deal.

They platted a town site on the land and named it in honor of John C. Fremont's most celebrated scout, Kit Carson. The following year, the discovery of the Comstock Lode brought

Carson City to life. It became a thriving trading post, freight and transportation center.

Even before Nevada became a state in 1864, Curry had determined that he would build a town on what was once known as Eagle Station. Curry and some friends purchased Eagle Station trading post and considerable ranch property from the financially strapped owner for $1,000, half paid in cash and the rest in a trade-off for a few mustang ponies.

The ever-visionary Curry had already determined that he would build his city and it would become a state capital, even though the state had not yet been born.

One account of the territory at the time is that if you gathered all the people in Eagle Valley, Carson Valley, and Washoe Valley, there'd probably be enough for three sets in a dance.

Abraham Curry was said to be a born organizer. He sketched out a plat for the town with streets surrounding a "Capitol Square." With this done, he hired, Jerry Long, a surveyor. To save his dwindling cash, he offered Long a full city block in the heart of the proposed town for his surveying services.

Long replied that he had no faith in the proposed town, and that he'd rather be owed the money than to own worthless land. The State Printing Office was eventually built on that some block turned down by Long.

Curry set aside four blocks of his new town for a plaza; an area he swore would one day be the location of the state capitol building. Dauntless in his planning, Curry next opened a brick-making business.

Carson City didn't exactly excite the imagination of property buyers. Lots were given away to anyone who would build on them. It is said that a pair of boots and $25 hard cash bought the block where the Methodist Church now stands, along with the parcel adjoining to the south.

Curry's partners lost any enthusiasm for the project they might have had. One of them sold Curry his one-fourth interest in the warm springs that had been discovered on the edge of town for a mustang pony and 25 pounds of butter.

The other partners, also unimpressed, simply gave their one-quarter shares to Curry, thus making him the sole owner of the warm springs, on which he later built a crude hotel a mile to the east of the town's center.

He called it the Warm Springs Hotel. When Carson City was selected as the territorial capital in 1861, the ever-ambitious Curry leased his hotel to the Legislature as a meeting hall.

Legislators also leased the Warm Springs Hotel to serve as the territorial prison, and named Curry as its first warden. The property was eventually purchased by the state and is still a part of the state prison system.

The winter of 1858-59 was the worst in years, and most ordinary men would have felt defeated. But it scarcely fazed Curry. Even though the snow piled high, stopping all travel westward because the mountain passes were blocked, Curry maintained his dream.

As luck would have it, the Comstock Lode was discovered in the hills beyond Eagle Valley, just a year after Curry had platted his town. Since Carson City was the closest center for shipping and supplies, the would-be city suddenly boomed.

Within two years, President Buchanan created the Territory of Nevada and Carson City was chosen as the Territorial Capitol.

Resources

1. With Curry's Compliments," by Doris Cerveri
2. "The Silver State," by James W. Hulse
3. "History of Nevada," by Russell R. Elliott

Chapter 11

The Territorial Enterprise

It took ample amounts of "valley tan" to lubricate both the two men and the equipment they struggled to install in the drafty shack, where snow filtered through the cracks.

The two men were printers attempting to install a second-hand Washington printing press. They cursed as they worked in the freezing temperatures of the shack.

Even the cannonball stove in the corner, glowing red with a fire of cottonwood logs, failed to heat the frigid room, or the men therein. The men thus resorted to frequent swigs on the "valley tan" bottle, which was described as "the sovereign remedy of the countryside."

Eventually, after liberal dousing of the liquor over stubborn parts of the machinery, as well as inside themselves, the men coaxed the ancient printing press into motion.

When the soberer of the two finally snatched a six-column sheet off the creaking press, it was the first copy of the first newspaper ever to be printed in Nevada. It would set the pattern for frontier journalism everywhere.

The two printers were W.L. Jernegan and Alfred James. The partners buttoned their frock coats and ran through the snow to the Stockade Bar to show the first copy of the paper to Isaac Roop, who settled the town of Susanville, California, and just happened to be in town. He was later Territorial Governor of Nevada.

Jernegan and James had lugged the printing press from Salt Lake by ox team to Mormon Station (now Genoa). There were fewer than 200 permanent residents at the time. It served as a freighting station on the emigrant route to California. It was also a staging depot where teamsters and draymen changed horses before tackling the ascent of the Sierra on the way to

Lake Tahoe, Strawberry, Sportsman's Hall, and, eventually, Hangtown.

The two men were at a loss as to what to call their newspaper. They had written a friend in the Mother Lode diggings of California, one Washington Wright, seeking suggestions. A return letter suggested the new enterprise in the then Territory of Western Utah, be called the Territorial Enterprise.

Both Jernegan and James were delighted with the suggestion and the Territorial Enterprise the newborn newspaper became. As no self-respecting newspaper during the times could come into being without a prospectus, the two owners wasted no time in running one up: It read:

A JOURNAL FOR THE EASTERN SLOPE

"The Undersigned very respectfully announce that they will commence on the first week of November next, 1858, at Carson City, Eagle Valley, the publication of a Weekly Independent Newspaper, entitled The Territorial Enterprise. It will industriously and earnestly be devoted to the advancement of everything pertaining to the beautiful country bounded on the West by the Sierra Nevadas and extending into and forming the Great Basin of the Continent.

The arrivals and departures of the Great Overland Mail and the incidents thereto will be carefully noted, and it will be the aim and Pride of the undersigned to print a Journal, which will be popular with and advantageous to every resident of the Utah Valleys. They, therefore, confidently rely upon the encouragement and liberality of their fellow residents."

W.L. Jernegan & Alfred James

As their luck would have it, the first issue of the Enterprise did not get printed during the first week of November. Mechanical problems were blamed. Although it was later learned the reason really was the printers were shy of type and did not have sufficient characters to piece out crossheads and display lines.

Neither was the first issue printed at Carson City. Because most of the traffic headed for the Sierra passes failed to go through Carson City, the owners moved the paper to Mormon Station.

Dan DeQuille, left, was on the Territorial Enterprise for 31 years. His fellow reporter, Mark Twain, was noted for his reporting on the Territorial Enterprise, but was often lazy and shuffled the work to DeQuille.

Apparently, no copy of the first issue of the Territorial Enterprise has survived. The mortality of such documents in an age of wooden buildings was fearfully high.

While Mark Twain was the more famous of the reporters at the Territorial Enterprise, it was actually Dan DeQuille that was the more substantial reporter of the two. Born William Wright, in Knox County, Ohio, in 1829, Will developed a wanderlust and headed to California and the gold country.

His efforts to scratch out a living prospecting were futile. He was successful in getting some of his letters published and one such letter caught the attention of Joseph Goodman, owner of the Territorial Enterprise in Virginia City.

Goodman decided to hire the young writer, who adopted the pen name of Dan DeQuille. It wasn't long after De Quille assumed his reporter's job that the Territorial Enterprise also hired another young letter writer.

This was the twenty-seven-year-old Samuel Langhorne Clemens, who would writer under the name of Mark Twain. He was paid twenty-five dollars per week.

Chic Di Francia, a printer, wrote in a biography of Dan DeQuille, "Because both men possessed enormous talent, it was a foregone conclusion that a friendly and competitive rivalry should exist between the two of them. As akin as the two were in talent, the similarity ended there."

Mark Twain lasted 21 months with the Territorial Enterprise, but Dan DeQuille pounded out copy for the *Enterprise* for thirty-one years. Dan developed a raging desire for alcohol and was fired from the newspaper, but was later reinstated when his daughter persuaded DeQuille to sober up.

As with many pioneer newspapermen, The Territorial Enterprise editors sometimes fell upon hard times. Hard currency was scarce and credit even scarcer. Subscribers often paid in trade goods, such as a hindquarter of venison, a dozen sage hens, or half a bear.

Resources

1. "A Paper is Born", History of the *Territorial Enterprise* by Lucius Beebe
2. "The Silver State," by James W. Hulse
3. "The Life and Times of Dan DeQuille," by Chic Di Francia

Chapter 12

The 'Richest Rail Line' in U.S.

It was called the "richest short line" in the United States.

At the start of 1869, Virginia City had a population of more than twenty thousand people. It was considered among the wealthiest cities in the world and one of the largest in the west.

When the town's glittering economy took a downturn, William Sharon, of the Bank of California, was quick to analyze the problem. Transportation of ore from mine to mill by teamsters was so costly that only the richest ores were processed. Costs needed to be lowered to protect the tremendous investment in mines, miles and cities.

Sharon hired mining engineer Isaac James to lay out a railroad from Virginia City through Gold Hill and down the mountain slopes to the mills on the Carson River, and thence a few miles westward to Carson City, the state capital.

Besides having a sharp eye for business opportunities, Sharon also had a lust for power. His plan was simple—extend cheap credit at half the going interest rate, then foreclose at the first opportunity. Within two years, Sharon, Ralston and the Bank of California had virtually every mine and mill on the Comstock under their control.

At one time, an average of 45 trains a day were running over the Virginia & Truckee Railroad to bring in supplies and lumber and to carry out ore. The railroad had twenty-one miles of some of the steepest, most twisting, and most expensive track ever laid in the country.

For the Fourth of July, 1892, V&T Engine No. 17 was decked out with colorful flags. (Nevada Historical Society)

Iron rails were brought in around Cape Horn from England. Locomotives were ordered from Booth's Union Iron Works in San Francisco and from Baldwin in Philadelphia, all 2-6-0 type Moguls.

The 0-6-0 was too rigid for the undulating track of the period, so in the early 1860s, a radial lead truck was added to the locomotive, creating a 2-6-0. (Earlier model 2-6-0s appeared in 1852, but the lead wheels were attached to the rigid locomotive frame and did not pivot on their own truck. Only a few were built.)

The swiveling lead truck was self-centering, and it was equalized in such a way that, together with the driving wheels, a three-point suspension system was created. This allowed the locomotive to traverse uneven track.

A silver spike was driven into a railroad tie at Carson City on September 28, 1869, completing the railroad route. The next day, the first train reached Gold Hill, greeted by waving flags and cheering crowds. Two months later, the first official passenger train reached Virginia City, on January 29, 1870.

Bank manager Sharon's lust for money and power came to a halt when a group of four men, John Mackay, James Fair, James Flood and William O'Brien assumed control of the Comstock. Their success at picking better producing mines allowed them to wrench control from Sharon and his associates.

The Bank of California, overburdened with bad loans on barren mines, went under. William Ralston was fired from his job as manager. He was found dead in San Francisco Bay soon after, believed to be the victim of suicide.

William Sharon continued to survive. He became a Senator from the State of Nevada in the Congress of the United States.

Competition from the trucking industry and the depletion of the Comstock ore, The Virginia and Truckee Railroad fought frantically to stay in business. It ran its tracks to Minden, Nevada from Carson City, to pick up agricultural and cattle freight from Douglas County.

In 1935, The Crown Point Trestle to Gold Hill was torn down in order to mine the ore beneath it. Soon after, Ogden Mills, the owner and steadfast fan of the Virginia & Truckee Railroad died. The railroad was placed in receivership.

In 1938, the board of directors announced its intention to close down the railroad. Equipment was sold off as antiques. In 1941, the tracks to Virginia City were finally torn out.

Resources

1. "Rebirth of the Virginia & Truckee R.R.," by Ted Wurm
2. "Nevada," by Gilman M. Ostrander
3. "The History of the Crookedest Short Line in America, the Virginia and Truckee Railroad," by Don Bush.

Chapter 13

West's last stage robbery

Being located at the back end of nowhere, Jarbidge seems an unlikely place for a stagecoach robbery.

Jarbidge, Nevada is the most isolated of all Nevada's prominent mining ghost towns. The robbery that took place there on December 5, 1916 was not just any stagecoach robbery. It goes down as the "last" horse drawn stagecoach holdup in the west.

Jarbidge is named after a Nez Perce word, "Jahabich," which means devil. It was the Indians' name for the nearby mountains, which they believed to be haunted by an evil giant.

The first white men in the area were ranchers. They raised horses, cattle and sheep. The ranchers supplied southern Idaho and northern Nevada with meat and wool.

When prospectors found placer gold in Jarbidge Canyon in 1909, it launched a stampede to Jarbidge, and a boomtown was born. Hopes ran high among prospectors.

"Before I had dug a hole ten feet deep in the property...I had been offered $2,000,000!" D.A. Bourne, of Boise, Idaho, told the Elko, Nevada Free Press (January 21, 1910). "Then I was given a chance to sell 100,000 shares for $1,000,000. But as there is ore valued at $27,000,000 in sight, I'm not selling."

The Elko *Independent* said, "On grades leading into Jarbidge Canyon the road averages not more than a foot wider than a wagon, and the slightest accident means a fall of thousands of feet. When this grade is filled with snow...the danger of passing over it can be better imagined than described."

On December 5, 1916, the incoming stage was long overdue. Those in Jarbidge knew it was not a good night to be traveling the hazardous mountain road.

Jarbidge about 1932.
(The Northwestern Nevada Museum, Elko)

Postmaster Scott Fleming feared the stage driver had had some kind of trouble. He asked Frank Leonard to ride out to see if he could spot the stagecoach and bring back the first class mail. Leonard returned without the mail or without having seen any sign of the overdue stagecoach.

It was a Mrs. Dexter, who lived on the north edge of town, who assured the citizen's that the stage had not gone off the grade. "Why, no," Mrs. Dexter said, "The stage didn't run off the grade—it passed my place about suppertime! The driver had his coat collar turned up about his face, and was huddled on the seat as if he was terribly cold."

A volunteer search party found the missing stagecoach in a dense clump of willows, 200 yards off the main road. The driver was slumped on the seat with a round black hole in the back of his head, the result of a gunshot.

The horses were still in their traces, tied to the clump of willows. The second-class mail sack had been slashed open and lay nearby, but the sack containing the first class mail was not to be seen. That sack is reported to have carried $3200 in cash, consigned to Crumley & Walker's Success Bar and Café.

Armed guards were posted to prevent anyone from leaving town. The next morning, it was determined that the killer had swung aboard the stagecoach at Crippen Grade, and shot the driver, Frank Searcy, in the back of the head.

Bloodstains in the road indicated that it was the murderer who was at the reins when the stage went past Mrs. Dexter's.

Footprints of a large man and paw prints of a dog were found leading from the stage to the river. The tracks went through the willows to a path that crossed a footbridge over the river and entered the business section of Jarbidge.

As the searchers tramped up and down the road looking for more clues, an old dog joined them. He was the type found in every mining camp, owned by nobody but everybody's friend. The paw prints in the snow also resembled those of the dog.

At one point, the dog suddenly darted into the willows and began pawing the snow. The dog soon uncovered the first-class mail pouch with its blood-smeared letters inside. Not found, however, was the parcel containing the gold coins.

Jarbidge residents knew that a local miner, Ben Kuhl was particularly fond of the dog, and allowed the cur to live in his cabin. In fact, the dog may have been Kuhl's only friend in the entire camp.

When the searchers found a bloodstained shirt under the bridge, similar to those worn by Kuhl, they figured they knew who had robbed the stage and killed the driver.

A trial was held in Elko. A web of circumstantial evidence connected Kuhl to the crime. A jury returned a verdict of murder in the first degree. Kuhl later confessed to the crime and got himself a commutation of his death sentence.

Kuhl claimed the holdup was actually a plan hatched by both he and stage driver Searcy. Searcy did not keep his end of the bargain and tried to kill him, Kuhl said, thus forcing Kuhl to kill Searcy instead.

The money taken in the robbery was never found. Some speculate that it still lies buried somewhere in the canyon near the lower end of town.

Resources

1. "Ghosts of the Glory Trail," by Nell Murbarger
2. "This Was Nevada," by Phillip I. Earl
3. "Ghost Towns of Nevada," by Donald C. Miller

Chapter 14

Balky burro founds Tonopah

Tonopah's main street in 1903. (Nevada State Historical Society)

Nevada lore indicates that Jim Butler picked up a rock to throw at a stubborn burro, but found gold and silver at Tonopah, Nevada instead.

According to the story, Jim Butler and his wife set out from Belmont, Nevada for the Southern Klondyke Mining District. It was their eighteenth day on the trail and they camped at a spring in a desolate spot at the foot of a hill. Tonopah is an Indian name that signifies a small spring.

Jim Butler (second from left) discovered rich ore that led to gold rush in Tonopah. (Tonopah Times-Bonanza)

Arising the next morning, they found their pack burros had strayed. Butler found them and herded them back toward camp. Exasperated at the slowness of one burro, Butler picked up a rock to hurl at the beast. He noticed that the stone was comprised of mineralized quartz. Nearby was a huge outcropping of the same material.

The Butlers gathered specimens and then continued on the remaining ten miles to Southern Klondyke.

When they showed their samples, the camp assayer snorted that they were probably worthless. He demanded an assaying fee to test them. The Butlers couldn't afford the fee.

On their return trip to Belmont, the Butlers gathered more samples from the outcropping. Butler then gave them to Tasker Oddie, Nye County district attorney, offering him a half interest if he could get an assay made.

Oddie was about as strapped for cash as the Butlers, but he took the specimens to Walter Gayheart, an Austin, Nevada

74

engineer, and offered him half of his interest to do the assay. When Gayheart made the assay, he found the ore contained $80 to $600 a ton in gold and silver.

Butler led his new partners to the site. They then staked a claim on every foot of ground anywhere near the outcropping. These included the Desert Queen, the Burro, the Mizpah, the Buckboard, and many other claims with colorful names.

Even the stone monuments they used to stake the claims were made of high-grade ore. From one fifteen-foot shaft, the group filled two wagons with ore. When processed in Austin, the net proceeds from the ore amounted to $600.

This began the big Tonopah rush. It drew new prospectors from all over the west to try their luck in the desert country, and it drew new investors from all over the country to take a fling at mining ventures.

The discovery at Tonopah closed the door on the long depression that had plagued the state of Nevada's mining industry since the decline of the Comstock. Within months, dozens of new discoveries were made in the southern part of the state.

During the nineteenth century, Nevada's economic life was based on "free mining"—that is, the unrestricted access to public land for those with the capital to exploit its riches.

Before 1872, the national government leased public lands to mine speculators who were required to pay a six percent royalty on their profits. This stimulated exploration all along Nevada's mining frontier.

Resources

1. "Desert Challenge," by Richard Gordon Lillard
2. "Nevada, readings and perspectives," edited by Michael S. Green and Gary E. Elliott
3. "History of Nevada," by Russell R. Elliott
4. "Death Valley & the Amargosa," by Richard E. Lingenfelter
5. "Nevada, A Guide to the Silver State," compile by Writer's Program Group, for Works Project Administration.

Chapter 15

Winnemucca

Chief Winnemucca

The first settler in what is now called Winnemucca was a Frenchman who set up a trading post in 1850 on the road to California. People crossing the river here with their oxcarts named the place French Ford. When a bridge was built in 1865, it became French Bridge.

A ferry was operating at the same time, which caused the bridge builder considerable discomfort because the ferryman charged only half that of the bridge crossing.

The settlement was at a key location on the river route in a very low saddle at the base of Winnemucca Mountain. The town was renamed Winnemucca, after the Paiute Indian Chief in 1863.

In 1862, J. Gianacca (who also built the bridge) conceived the idea of building a 90-mile canal between Golconda and a projected mill city. The canal would carry ore from the district to central smelters and provide waterpower to run them.

By 1865, 30 miles of canal had been built, but then Gianacca began having trouble raising money for the rest of the construction, particularly since the railroad was constructing a line along the same course. Nearly 60 miles of canal was built but water never reached Mill City.

Winnemucca was still something of a frontier settlement in 1900 when three strangers rode down the dusty main street. Hitching their horses behind the First National Bank, they hoisted a last drink in a nearby saloon, and then sauntered into the bank.

Within minutes the strangers walked out the rear door, remounted, and rode away with $32,640. Before disappearing, they fired their guns in the air to inform the town that Butch Cassidy and his boys had been there.

Winnemucca in the 1930s

The gang rode along the river where a relay of fresh horses was waiting. These horses were also stolen—from the president of the bank. While a posse chased the robbers, they were able to escape into central Wyoming. The money was never recovered.

Winnemucca is the county seat of Humboldt County. The name is of Paiute origin.

One story is that when the first white trappers reached the lower end of the Humboldt River in the late 1840s, they met a young Indian who claimed to be a chief. The young man was in love and Paiute custom dictated that he dispense with one moccasin as a sign that his heart was not free.

The white trappers dubbed him "One Moccasin," using the Paiute word for footwear, *mau-cau*. This was later corrupted into Winnemucca. The name has since been interpreted to mean various things, such as "bread giver," "the giver," and "charitable man"

Lee Winnemucca, son of old Chief Winnemucca, verified the one-shoe origin of the name. But Chief Harry Winnemucca, of the Pyramid Lake Paiute Tribe, a great grandson of the old chief, says that family tradition indicates his ancestor lost a shoe while fleeing from a cavalryman on the Forty Mile Desert.

Winnemucca's quiet attitude of today hasn't changed a great deal from its placid beginnings.

One of Winnemucca's most exciting times in the past was when residents were given a citation because of their wandering milk cows. When the automobile, electricity and the telephone reached Winnemucca so did city ordinances.

In Winnemucca's early days, residents simply dumped their garbage over the back fence and into the alleys. The garbage problem was taken care of by allowing pigs to run loose.

While the pigs were fattening, it wasn't really curing the garbage problem, as the waste from the pigs simply increased the dilemma.

Soon after the 1900s, it was considered uncivilized to allow pigs to run loose, and an ordinance was passed making it illegal to do so.

It was only natural that other animal ordinances would follow. It soon became illegal to turn cows loose in the streets of Winnemucca. The owners of the wandering cows were taking advantage of free grazing in between milking times.

A city ordinance was passed in August 1912 requiring residents inside the city limits of Winnemucca to keep their cows penned. The word was a little slow in getting to some residents.

Officials started enforcing the ordinance three days later. When it came time for milking, townspeople found their cows were missing. When they went to the Constable, they learned that he had them confined to enforce the ordinance.

The *National Miner* newspaper, on August 16, 1912, reported:

> *Yesterday's offense being the first, and it being evident that some people were not familiar with the ordinance, no fine was imposed, but the owners were required to appear before Justice Dunn this morning, and the ordinance was read to them.*

The town was not one of illiterate residents. By 1871, Winnemucca had a newspaper with a circulation of 200, and it began a public library the same year.

In 1928, the library changed its rules regarding its use. The newspaper, *The Silver State*, reported that to borrow a book, a person simply gave the librarian their name and address, and paid five cents for the first book. There were no further charges until the person had checked out and returned a total of 24 books.

So much for another day in Winnemucca.

Resources
1. "Nevada, A Guide to the Silver State," compiled by workers of the Writer's Program of the Works Projects Administration in the State of Nevada.
2. "This Was Nevada," by Phillip I. Earl
3. "Marden Historical Research"

Chapter 16

Las Vegas: once a way-station

Las Vegas in 1905.   (Nevada Historical Society)

A Mexican trader named Antonio Armijo was leading a sixty-man party on a mission to establish a trade route to Los Angeles in 1829. He veered from the accepted route, and camped on Christmas Day about 100 miles northeast of present-day Las Vegas.

A scouting party rode west in search of water. Rafael Rivera, a young Mexican scout, left the main party and ventured into the unexplored desert. Rivera became lost in the Virgin River country and was gone for twelve days.

He eventually arrived at the point where present-day Henderson, Nevada is located. From an elevated spot, he gazed at the lush green Las Vegas Valley.

Fur trapper Jedediah Smith is said to have crossed the Colorado River near Needles in 1826. Smith is credited with opening a trail across the deserts of the great Southwest to the Pacific Coast. This eventually became "The Old Spanish Trail."

The trail has a cruel history. Along with legitimate commerce, it also brought illicit trade in both humans and horseflesh. Unscrupulous traders captured and traded for Indian children to sell as slaves at either terminus of the trail.

Fourteen years after Rivera's discovery of Las Vegas Springs, John C. Fremont led an overland expedition west and camped there May 13, 1844. Mormon settlers from Salt Lake City traveled to Las Vegas to protect the Los Angeles-Salt Lake City mail route and in 1855 began building a fort that measured 150-foot on each side. The fort was built from sun-dried bricks made of clay soil and grass, known today as adobe.

Frontier life in Southern Nevada was harsh. The settlers were isolated from other communities by miles of barren desert. There was little if any relief from the heat, hordes of insects were common, and grasshoppers devoured their crops.

It was railroad developers who decided the Las Vegas Valley would be a good location for a railroad stop and for a town. Work on the first railroad grade into Las Vegas began the summer of 1904. The tent town of Las Vegas sprouted saloons, stores and boarding houses.

In 1905, a public auction of business lots and home sites was held and the city of Las Vegas came into existence. The new community of Las Vegas was a part of Lincoln County, which comprised 18,576 square miles, and one of the largest political subdivisions in the nation. The county seat was located 150 miles from Las Vegas at Pioche.

A plea for home rule was made to the state legislature and Clark County, named after Senator William A. Clark, was born.

Nevada was the first state to legalize casino-style gambling. It was also the last western state to outlaw gaming in the first decade of the 20th Century.

At midnight, October 1, 1910, a strict anti-gambling law became effective in Nevada. It even forbid the western custom of flipping a coin for the price of a drink.

The Nevada State Journal in Reno reported:

Stilled forever is the click of the roulette wheel, the rattle of dice and the swish of cards.

Forever-lasted less than three weeks in Las Vegas. Gamblers quickly set up underground games where patrons who knew the proper password gambled day and night.

In 1931, the Nevada Legislature approved a legalized gambling bill. Today, more than 43 percent of the state general fund is fed by gambling tax revenue.

Resources
1. "Nevada, The Silver State," published by Western State Historical Publishers.
2. "Nevada, Official Bicentennial Book"
3. "History of Nevada," by Russell R. Elliott

Chapter 17

Tuscarora, a boomtown

Tuscarora as it looked in 1880. (The Northeastern Nevada Museum)

Tuscarora is one of those towns that tried to roar but just couldn't make it.

"Tuscarora began as most western mining towns, by rumor," said Howard Hickson, a Nevada history chronicler.

During the twenty-year stretch from 1870 to 1890, Tuscarora produced $40,000,000 in silver. It is now a still-living ghost town, located 52 miles from Elko, Nevada.

Old timers say C.M. Benson, a prospector who came to the area during the gold strike, probably named the town. Benson had been a sailor on the United States gunboat *Tuscarora*. The gunboat had been named after an eastern seaboard tribe of Indians.

Credit for the gold strike at Tuscarora is given to John and Steven Beard, who, in 1867, learned from a trader that an Indian had told of gold found in a creek there.

For a time, Tuscarora looked like it would really boom. It had two newspapers, which merged in less than a year to one, the *Tuscarora Times-Review.*

In one report, the newspaper called attention to a message from telegraph company headquarters in San Francisco. The message warned that the telegraph lines to Tuscarora would be taken away if Tuscarora-Elko teamsters didn't quit chopping down the poles to use as fuel.

Chinese workmen came to Tuscarora to work on the railroad. Plans were to extend the Nevada Central Railroad from Battle Mountain through Tuscarora and on to Idaho, but the plans were never completed.

The Chinese worked much of the placer ground during the 1870s, usually on a royalty basis of ten percent of the bullion recovered. There were up to 2,500 Chinese in the diggings at one time.

They could only mine during the spring and summer, when water was available. During the fall and winter, the Chinese cut sagebrush to fuel the steam plants in nearby silver mills.

One of the last survivors of the Chinese that worked in the placer mines was Yen Tin. In 1934, some youngsters playing in Tuscarora found $1,200 worth of gold nuggets that had been hidden near Yen Tin's cabin. Yen Tin had died in 1927.

Tuscarora was flooded with hordes of prospectors, merchants, professional people, con men, hurdy gurdy girls and outright crooks, said history writer Hickson.

Streets and alleys were declared public highways to prevent men from staking out claims on the thoroughfares. Miners' wages went up to four dollars a day.

Excitement in Tuscarora then died down and residents settled in for quiet and leisurely living. They did get a scare in 1963 when state health officials found the town's water supply was being contaminated by cows.

Resources

1. "Tuscarora Never Died," By Howard Hickson and Tony Primeaux, Nevada Historical Society Quarterly.
2. "Ghost Towns of Nevada," by Don C. Miller
3. "Nevada, the Silver State," by Western States Historical Publishers

Chapter 18

Nevada's singing sand dunes

Scientists report that some sand dunes in Nevada, California and Hawaii emit acoustical energy when disturbed.

The sounds are described variously as "roaring," "booming," "squeaking," "singing," and "musical." Some have compared the latter to musical instruments such as the kettledrum, zither, tambourine, bass violin, and a trumpet. Other scientists, perhaps with a different musical ear, have described the tones as more like a foghorn or low-flying propeller-driven aircraft.

These musical sand dunes have been found at Sand Mountain, Nevada, Kelso Dunes, California, and Barking Sands, Kauai.

Reporting on the singing and booming sand dunes were Dennis T. Trexler, division of earth sciences, University of Nevada, Reno, and Wilton N. Melhorn, department of Geosciences, Purdue.

Four additional sites emitting the booming sounds are Eureka Dunes and Panamint Dunes in California, and Crescent Dunes and Big Dune in Nevada. One thing the researchers have found is that all sound-producing desert dune sands are medium grained.

"The sand must be dry, because as little as 0.1 percent moisture makes a marked difference in sound producing capability, and one percent moisture permits only feeble sound production," said R.W. Fairbridge, in his Encyclopedia of Geomorphology.

Sand Mountain and singing sand dunes.
(Tom Schweich)

These singing sand dunes are believed to form and exist under very special and limited conditions. Sand particles are apparently honed by the wind until they are well rounded, extremely smooth, and highly polished (frosted).

Until recently, scientists were unsure of what caused the audible sounds. More recently, they have found that the internal shearing of sand grains during avalanches down a dune slope produces the booming sound.

In their paper, published in California Geology, Trexler and Melhorn said acoustic emissions from Crescent Dunes, Nevada in July 1976 were so loud and realistic that the authors' field assistant was searching the skies for a turboprop aircraft.

The Crescent Dunes complex is in western Nye County on the east side of Big Smoky Valley, approximately ten miles Northeast of Tonopah. From Tonopah, travel west on U.S. Highway 50 and 95 for approximately 2.1 miles to a paved county road to Anaconda's Molybdenum mine; turn right (north) and go 10 miles. The dune is visible on the right and a sign denotes the turnoff.

In their California Geology report, the scientists note that the dunes rise only 230 feet above the surrounding terrain. The sand in the dunes is believed to come from the now dry bed of prehistoric Lake Tonopah.

The reporting scientists came up with some specific observations regarding the "singing" or "booming" sands.

1. Sands that have traveled the farthest in a particular dune field have the greatest potential to produce acoustical energy.
2. High dunes, with steep, quasi-stable slip faces that are easily put in motion produce the best sounds.
3. Dunes that contain medium-sized sand grains, which are very-well-sorted to well-sorted, are the best prospects for production of acoustical energy.
4. The sands must be dry and meteorological conditions must provide low humidity.
5. Well-rounded, frosted sand grains derived from long-distance transport, or multiple generations of sand movement resulting from variable azimuth wind direction appear best suited to the production of booming sounds.
6. Vehicular traffic on dune surfaces tends to degrade the ability of the sands to produce sounds under natural conditions.

The Legend of the Singing Sands

(As told by Mary Holliday, a published writer and Nevada history teacher, in "Nevada, Official Bicentennial Book"

"Somewhere in my early childhood, while growing up in Churchill County, I heard about the singing sands of Sand Mountain. Perhaps that story began during the Mesozoic era when the mountains were being thrust up in the Great Basin. It was a time when plesiosaurs and ichthyosaurs of the oceans became trapped in an inland sea.

"The ichthyosaurs became beached and, being heavy of body, collapsed under their own weight. But the plesiosaurs, being slender sea monsters, slithered to safety into ancient Lake Lahontan. A pair of these long-necked serpents survived the waters of Walker Lake when the violent winds came to dry the land and change the shape of the earth.

"While heavy winds were lifting sand from the shores of Walker Lake and depositing it at Sand Mountain, the serpents were safe in the depths of the desert lake. Day after day the storm raged on while they waited, dozed, and waited. But— hearing the music of the wind, the female was lured from the quiet safety by her desire to roll in the waves and play. Many times they had risen together and in delight had ridden the mighty waves that leaped high into the air. Together they would twine their lengthy, fifty-foot bodies against the pull of the storm and glory in their combined strength against the forces.

"But without the protection of the huge male's weight, a whirlwind caught her and swirled her into the vortex of the storm that left the sandy shores rough with rocks. Along with tons of sand, she was spun away and plunged beneath the weight of Sand Mountain many ridges to the north.

"Now she moans for her mate of long ago and the blue waters of Walker Lake and the pure joy of swimming free. No longer does a sweet spring at the base of Sand Mountain gush forth at twilight to wet her tongue; and while the winds blow, she twists and turns in torment with thirst. It is for her need that the sands sing to rest her agony."

Chapter 19

Reno: *Nevada's 'Biggest Little City'*

Reno in 1906.   (Nevada Historical Society)

Nevada was only a bridge between Salt Lake City and San Francisco until the town of Reno was born.

Truckee Meadows was on the emigrant trail and well known for its water, game, and grass, features that attracted permanent settlers in 1850.

One of these settlers was C.W. Fuller who built ferry and then a bridge over the Truckee River. The site became known as Fuller's Crossing.

The bridge eventually washed out and he sold the now unstable business to Myron C. Lake, who improved the bridge and built a hotel and trading post to accommodate travelers. It became known as Lake's Crossing. His toll road collections ran as high as $2,500 a day.

By the time the Central Pacific was ready to cross into Nevada, Lake held ownership to a large section of land in the path of the railroad. He struck a bargain with Charles Crocker, superintendent of construction for the railroad.

Lake agreed to donate 400 acres of land north of the river to the Central Pacific for a town site, on condition that Crocker would build a railroad station there.

Crocker named the new town *Reno*, in honor of General Jesse L. Reno, a Union officer killed at the battle of South Mountain, Maryland, in 1862.

The town of Reno became a major supply center for the Comstock Mines. The town's position was made even more secure when the Virginia and Truckee Railroad was extended to Reno in 1872.

When Nevada became a state, the seat of Washoe County was designated as Washoe City, then the biggest town in Washoe Valley. Like most railroad towns, Reno brought pressure to become the county seat of government. Reno literally took the county seat away from Washoe City after a bitter fight

The first building lot in Reno was sold at an auction held by the Central Pacific Railroad. The lot sold for $600, and a combination saloon and gambling hall was built on it. There has never been anything on that lot since other than a bar or casino.

THIS SALE WILL AFFORD A GRAND OPPORTUNITY
for favorable investments in town lots suitable for all kinds of business and trades. The depot being permanently located at this point will give the town of RENO a commanding position of vast importance to secure the trade of Nevada and that portion of California lying east of the Sierras, and will be the natural market for the produce of the rich agricultural valleys north.

Situated on the Truckee River, affording water power unsurpassed in the United States, and where the VIRGINIA AND TRUCKEE railroad connects with the PACIFIC, it is unnecessary to enumerate the many advantages this town will possess as the center of immense milling and manufacturing operations.

R E N O !
VIRGINIA STATION,
— ON THE —
PACIFIC RAILROAD!
AUCTION SALE OF TOWN LOTS
— IN —
THIS NEWLY LOCATED TOWN
WILL TAKE PLACE ON
SATURDAY, MAY 9, 1868.

Nevada's legislature made gambling illegal in 1910. The fight against gambling grew when Nevada's first governor, H.G. Blasdel took office. He continually vetoed legislation having anything to do with legalized gambling.

In 1869, however, the legislature legalized gambling over the governor's veto. Reformers had little success in attacking gambling thereafter. Even when gambling was forbidden there was a great deal of it going on in "underground" clubs with watchmen at the doors.

Reno became famous for an industry that had nothing to do with gambling, finance, crime or politics. The town became the "divorce capital" of the nation. In 1906, Laura Corey ended her 21-year marriage to the president of U.S. Steel by divorcing him in Reno.

The divorce trade attracted people from all walks of life. The Nevada residency requirement was only six months to get a divorce. It was later dropped to only six weeks. It brought movie stars and society's elite, as well as the common couples simply wanting to part ways.

Mary Pickford divorced Owen Moore there in order to marry Douglas Fairbanks. The divorce traffic prompted the major wire services to keep full-time reporters near the Washoe County Courthouse.

Reno's first big casino operators were Raymond I. "Pappy" Smith, who established "Harold's Club", and William Harrah, who opened a series of bingo parlors before building casinos at both Reno and Tahoe. Both Smith and Harrah came to Reno in the mid 1930s.

> "It wasn't uncommon for Mr. Smith personally to make refunds to customers in amounts that were almost staggering. For instance, $350,000 in one particular year was refunded to people who had spent the grocery money. If anyone was found in that predicament, they were to be sent to Mr. Smith." (Leslie Kofoed, Harold's Club executive)

Smith was said to be generous to a fault, returning money lost by ignorant gamblers with no means to get out of town.

Reno came into the limelight nationally when it staged a prizefight between former champion Jim Jeffries and Jack Johnson, the first black person to hold the heavyweight title.

Fans poured into town long before the match. Every hotel room in town was booked and there were miles of special trains and sleeping cars lining the tracks.

Jeffries was expected to win the fight, but Jeffries was not up to the task in the blazing July sun. Blacks began celebrating Johnson's victory across the country, and in the riots that ensued in many towns, at least seven people died.

Resources

1. "History of Nevada," by Russell R. Elliott
2. "Touring Nevada," by Mary Ellen and Al Glass

96

3. Reno Chamber of Commerce
4. "Reno," by Barbara and Myrick Land
5. "History of Nevada," by Robert Laxalt

Chapter 20

The Chinese in Nevada

Chinese immigrants began arriving in Nevada after 1849. Just as the rest of the gold rush pioneers, they were seeking wealth in the gold mines.

They met with racial hatred almost immediately. They were subjected to unfair laws as well as physical violence. State statutes forbade the Chinese from owning property.

Chinese gold miner
(Nevada Historical Society)

More than 3,000 Chinese were counted in Nevada in the census of 1870. More than 5,000 were counted ten years later. Most of them had left their wives and families in South China to work for a few years in the "Mountain of Gold."

White miners singled out Chinese miners for such frequent attacks that that they were sometimes driven out of the industry and relegated to service occupations such as laundering and cooking.

The Chinese were prohibited by state statute from owning property. During one political convention, the local platform called for the prohibition of Chinese and Japanese immigration.

It was during the 1867 to 1869 period when the Central Pacific Railroad was being built that many of the Chinese immigrants arrived. They were excellent railroad workers, a fact that made them even more unwelcome by their white counterparts.

Central Pacific Railroad workers laid tracks across Nevada in 1867 and 1868. Chinese workers were used.   (Nevada Historical Society)

Mining unions saw the Chinese as threats to the union and as tools of corporate monopolists. The Chinese were excluded from union membership and were thus denied employment in the mines, which were closed union shops.

There were two unions at the Comstock, the Virginia City Miner's Union and the Gold Hill Miner's Union. In 1869, the unions feared that Chinese labor would be brought into the Comstock. The unions joined together in a formal appeal to their members, asking them to approve sending delegates to a union meeting in Virginia City.

The object of the proposed meeting was to maintain wages at a satisfactory standard and "prevent the firm seating of Chinese labor in our midst." The convention never met and the Chinese labor threat continued to be a thorn in the side of the Caucasian miners.

At one point, 350 miners demonstrated against Chinese laborers being used in the building of the Virginia and Truckee Railroad. The union's opposition was strong enough to force

100

railroad management to sign an agreement guaranteeing that no Chinese would be employed within the limits of Virginia City and Gold Hill.

During Nevada's Comstock era, the Chinese suffered innumerable indignities and were often the targets of anti-Chinese riots.

Chinatown, Reno about 1900.   (Nevada Historical Society)

Perhaps no atrocity against the Chinese was greater than that committed in Reno, an event fully sanctioned by the Grand Jury, the police chief, the fire chief, and the city engineer.

This was the burning of Reno's Chinatown. Some say it was without warning to the 150 Chinese who lived there.

Chinatown occupied valuable property east of Virginia Street and north of the Truckee River. The city wanted this property— so without adieu, they destroyed Chinatown, leaving families homeless at the beginning of winter.

Officials argued that the razing of Chinatown probably saved the community from a major epidemic. Chinatown, they said, was "unsanitary" and an eyesore.

101

Dr. A.M. Robinson, chairman of the city's Board of Health, testified that Reno's Chinatown was indeed a city hazard. Waste from the slum was running into the Truckee River, and cesspools of standing water and large yellow rats scurrying through the alleyways were potential causes of disease.

Since the Chinese did not own the land, they had virtually no recourse against the city.

Resources
1. "The Sagebrush State," by Michael W. Bowers
2. "History of Nevada," by Russell R. Elliott
3. "Reno," by Barbara and Myrick Land
4. Reno News and Review, November 1, 1908
5. "Nevada, Official Bicentennial Book," Edited by Stanley W. Paher

Chapter 21

Queho: *A tale of murder and intrigue*

A tale persists in Nevada history about an Indian named Queho.

There are contradictory stories about Queho's origins and early years. One is that he was a Paiute and the other that he belonged to an Arizona tribe but lived for a time among the Paiutes near Las Vegas.

Tribal leaders kept few records, so little is known about Queho's early years. Some reports place Queho's birth around 1880 at Cottonwood Island, near Nelson, Nevada on the Colorado River. There are some who said Queho was cruelly ridiculed as a child because of his infirmity.

It is known that he was raised on a reservation in Las Vegas. He worked as a ranch laborer and as a wood gatherer in the mining camps, He was known for his sullenness, as well as his quick temper.

Queho's story surfaced again after, lying dormant for years, when prospectors Charles Kenyon and Art Schroeder noticed a man-made barricade in front of a shallow cave in the face of a high canyon wall.

Closer investigation revealed the skeleton of an Indian. Near the skeleton were a loaded shotgun, a bow, steel-tipped arrows, bullet molds, and other odds and ends.

When a Clark County coroner's jury investigated, it was determined the body was that of Queho (pronounced *kway-oh* or *kay-o*. It was believed that Queho had killed 23 people—mostly Caucasian and at least one Paiute—from 1910 until his death about 1920.

One tale is that Queho murdered a Paiute Indian in some intra-tribal row over the methods used by a medicine man.

The posse that recovered Queho's remains stands at the mouth of his cave hideout. From left, Clarke Kenyon, Frank Wait, Queho's remains, and Art Schroeder.   (University of Nevada)

Queho is also accused of murdering Hy Bohn, a shopkeeper. He broke both of the man's arms with a pick handle, stunned him with a blow to the head, and then fled into the mountains southwest of Las Vegas.

Queho's known history begins in 1910 when he killed a woodcutter for his supplies. Shortly after, he killed the guard of the Gold Bug Mine near Eldorado. He was linked to various crimes by his tracks, which had unusual characteristics. He dragged one leg as a result of an early injury.

Local lawmen thought they could easily track Queho down, believing he was little more than an ignorant savage. Queho stole a horse from a man named Cox and the chase really began.

The operator of the Eldorado mine, James Babcock, a lawyer educated in Washington, D.C, led the search party. Also in the tracking party was an Indian agent named DeCrevecoer.

Queho's trail then became somewhat obscure for several years. He was blamed for the disappearance of several lone prospectors and miners.

One story from the Las Vegas Review Journal told the following story:

> One afternoon, a local miner came into a clearing near Timber Mountain and there, seated on a rock, his .30-30 rifle across his lap, was the "ignorant savage" himself. Fred Pine, who had known Queho in Las Vegas, greeted him in his most amiable tone of voice.
>
> Queho responded in kind, no animosity in his voice. So they did lunch. Pine dug out a bag of sandwiches, and passed some of them to Queho. When he had finished, Queho told Pine that he, too, wanted to share his lunch, and produced a dried rodent of some sort. Pine gracefully declined.
>
> After about a half-hour, he decided to try to make an exit. He said good-bye and walked away, expecting to be felled at any moment. He wasn't.
>
> "I guess he just wasn't in a killing mood that day," Pine later recalled.

Newspaper reports show Queho did get in a killing mood again in 1913. A 100-year-old blind Indian known as Canyon Charlie was found dead, a pickax wound in his head.

The Las Vegas Review Journal reported, "Charlie's meager supply of food was gone; mute testimony of the terrifying fact that this ghost-like maniac would kill for anything—or nothing—since he might easily have stolen the old man's belongings without resorting to murder."

Some believe that Queho didn't do this murder at all because Canyon Charlie was a friend and confidant.

Two more miners, who were working claims at Jenny Springs on the Arizona side of the river, were next found dead. They were shot in the back and their personal belongings taken.

Then, an Indian woman, still clutching the bundle of wood she had been gathering, was found dead. She hadn't been robbed, but the blame was laid on Queho.

As Queho hysteria grew, so did the rewards for his capture. A reward of $2,000 was eventually offered.

In 1919, Queho attempted to steal food from the home of Ned Douglas near Eldorado. He shot Maude Douglas, the miner's wife when she walked into the kitchen and surprised him. This killing of a woman roused the feelings of officials, causing them to take up the chase for the villain.

The trail led up the Colorado to St. Thomas, now buried by the northern arm of Lake Mead, across to the Arizona side of the river, then back down the Nevada side.

Near St. Thomas, two prospectors were killed in savage style. Two days later, two more men and two boys were found murdered on the opposite side of the river near Black Canyon.

Seven killings in all took place during this period, with Queho's characteristic footprints showing quite clearly at each site.

Some people said Queho killed for food and other supplies. But at least one man who knew him said the Indian was far too expert in the capture of game to kill from hunger. Sometimes he took the shoes of his victims.

For months, men from both Nevada and Arizona attempted to follow his tracks. The Clark County sheriff got close on a number of occasions, finding campfires that were not yet cold.

Clark County Sheriff Joe Keate was an ardent Queho chaser. In the early 1930s, he was sent to Southern Nevada in quest of Queho while serving as state policeman.

The hunt for Queho finally ended in February 1940 when his mummified body was found in the mountain cave.

Resources

1. "Nevada, A Guide to the Silver State," compiled by the Writers' Program of the Work Projects Administration.
2. Las Vegas Review Journal
3. "Queho, The Renegade Indian," by Harry Reid and K.J. Evans

Chapter 22

Virginia City's 'Barbary Coast'

Almost as quick to arrive at a new gold strike as the miners were the voluptuous and delightful dance hall girls. While these ladies of the evening were not all beautiful and comely, in the eyes of the women-hungry miners, they were all welcome.

When Virginia City was born by the discovery of the Comstock, saloons sprouted faster than did miner's tents. And as soon as there was a saloon or a boarding house opened, it usually had prostitutes and dance-hall girls ready to give pleasure to the miners, all for a price that is.

Makeshift "cribs" quickly sprang up along "D" Street in Virginia City. There were high-class prostitutes, simple streetwalkers and women that had succumbed to alcohol or drug addiction all trying to get their pinch of gold dust from the miners' poke.

Julia Bulette, toast of Virginia City.

One section of "C" street was called "The Barbary Coast," adapted from the famous Barbary Coast in San Francisco. In a short time, the Barbary Coast in Virginia City was said to be twice as evil as the one in San Francisco, which was certainly no slouch in that category.

107

In 1863, Virginia City's Board of Aldermen passed an ordinance against houses of prostitution in an effort to cut down the lawlessness and debauchery attached to them.

The Virginia Evening Bulletin reported:

> The Board of Aldermen, at their meeting on the 13th, took action upon the many nuisances at present existing in our midst in the shape of houses of ill fame, and passed a very stringent ordinance against their existence in so central a part of town.
>
> We are glad to see the Board have some regard for the morality of the city, and their recent action has met the hearty approval of our citizens.
>
> The first section of the ordinance says that it shall be unlawful to open or maintain any house of ill-repute or brothel in the district of this city west of D street, or south of Sutton Avenue or north of Mill street; and the second section sets forth that any owner of a house or property included in the district in this city who shall let, hire or rent his or her property for the occupancy of women of bad or immoral character, shall give and pay to the city five hundred dollars. Some may consider this rather stringent, but we do not, and we hope to see the provisions of the ordinance carried into effect.

The ordinance had hardly been passed when a fire swept through the area, destroying a number of buildings that were occupied by prostitutes. It wasn't long before the ladies simply moved to other quarters outside the area restricted to them by the city ordinance.

In 1874, The Virginia and Truckee Railroad Company purchased the burned out property to continue their railroad and to build a depot. The company graded the property to locate warehouses, depot premises and sidetracks.

The prostitutes still in the area were warned to vacate their houses, but many stayed, rent free, until the last moment. They always found new buildings to occupy and carry on their trade. The citizens did continue to complain about the lewd women and shameless men occupying the dens of inequity in their midst but other than an occasional arrest, little was done to move the ladies of the evening out of town.

One of the most famous of the Virginia City prostitutes was Julia Bulette. Some stories said she migrated to the United States from London, England in 1849. Other writers say Julia immigrated to Louisiana where she married. She then left her husband and entered prostitution. Still other writers say she was born near Natchez, Mississippi, and worked as a prostitute in New Orleans.

John Millian, a Frenchman, murdered her in 1867 by strangulation. There were blows to the right temple and right eye.

Julia's previous life took on an almost enchanting version of how she lived in Virginia City, all or most of it untrue, according to Guy Rocha, Nevada State Archivist.

One author depicted Julia as wearing silk, velvet, and sable furs. Shortly after her arrival in Virginia City, the fiction writers wrote, she was making $1,000 a night and accepted payment in the form of bars of bullion.

Rocha said, "Absolute nonsense and pure poppy-cock! While Bulette had seen better days, she died in debt, according to estate records, her bills exceeding her assets.

Writers also described her as a "beautiful and willowy woman who seemed to float as she walked." Rocha sets the record straight. "She was neither wealthy, beautiful, willowy, nor did the rather heavy-set woman seemingly float when she walked."

Julia Bulette lived and worked out of a small rented cottage near the corner of D and Union streets in Virginia City's entertainment district. Early writers elevated Julia to the position of madam and "the queen" of Virginia City's sporting row."

One thing that is certain, Julia became a favorite among Virginia City's Fire Engine Company No. 1. The firemen, according to some accounts, elected her an honorary member "in return for numerous favors and munificent gifts bestowed by her upon the company."

Julia's death brought her more notoriety than did her activities as a prostitute.

Resources

1. "Harlots, Hurdies & Spirited Women of Virginia City, Nevada," by Barbara Hegne
2. Nevada Online Encyclopedia
3. Nevada State Archivist Guy Rocha.

Chapter 23

From Rags to Riches to Rags

Octavius Decatur Gass was a failure as a prospector in Arizona and California. He decided to move on to the Muddy River, located 65 miles east of Las Vegas Springs.

It was when he decided to take a look at the abandoned Mormon Fort in the area that now comprises Las Vegas that Gass's fortunes turned. The original settlement had been developed in 1855 by thirty missionaries sent there by Brigham Young, the head of the Mormon Church in Salt Lake City. Political infighting among the Mormon leadership ended the venture.

O.D. Gass

Along with two partners, Nathaniel Lewis and Lewis Cole, Gass set about rebuilding and improving the Mormon Fort to provide a way station for travelers on the Old Spanish Trail.

The three partners had 640 acres. Gass held ownership to 160 of those acres. By 1872, he had bought out his partners and owned the entire ranch and old fort outright.

The ranch produced grain, vegetables and Mexican pink beans, which Gass used to pay his Indian ranch hands. Local Indians were accustomed to a diet heavy with mesquite beans and regarded the plump Mexican beans a rare delicacy.

Gass also grew apples, peaches, figs and apricots, along with horses and cattle.

Farming was not Gass' only interest. He also invested money in the first seaport on the Colorado River at Callville, Nevada. Gass promoted the town heavily in Arizona newspapers, hoping it would become a major shipping port. The arrival of the transcontinental railroad in Utah defeated that effort, however.

When Gass acquired his ranch, it was located in the Territory of Arizona, and Gass sat on the territorial legislature. Gass was considered well spoken and well liked, even among the Paiutes, whose tongue he took the time to learn.

In 1866, congress passed a bill that moved Nevada's eastern border several miles further east. The Gass property thus was now located in the Territory of Nevada.

Getting deeper and deeper in debt, Gass eventually mortgaged his Las Vegas Ranch, as he called it, to William Knapp for $3,000. He then left for California to obtain bullion with which to pay off Knapp.

Gass eventually lost his Nevada properties. Nevada was demanding two years' back taxes. Gass moved to Redlands, California to be with his son. He died December 10, 1924.

Sadly, history has nearly forgotten the man that once owned what is now Las Vegas, except for a street in downtown that still carries his name.

Resources
1. "Nevada, Readings and Perspectives," edited by Michael S. Green and Gary E. Elliott.
2. "Nevada, A Guide to the Silver State," compiled by Writers' Program of the Works Projects Administration.
3. "O.D. Gass", Las Vegas Review-Journal, by K.J. Evans (Web Site)

Chapter 24

E Clampus Vitus

The Ancient and Honorable Order of E Clampus Vitus (there is never a period after the E) was founded back in the gold rush days.

Pinning down the history and true purpose of these *"Clampers"* is about as difficult as lassoing a snake. Yet, this organization that began as a spoof on other fraternal lodges and secret societies still exists with a rousing membership across the country.

The Ancient and Honorable Order of E Clampus Vitus

As one Clamper historian wrote, "The early meetings of E Clampus Vitus were devoted so completely to drinking and carousing that none of the Clampers was ever in any condition to keep minutes, let alone remember what had happened the next day!"

The Clampers claimed that all their members were officers and "of equal indignity", but that some, such as the Clampatriarch and the Noble Grand Humbug, were more equal than others were.

According to tradition, a person could join E Clampus Vitus by invitation only and then was expected to endure an elaborate and grueling initiation ceremony. Sometimes the new initiate was blindfolded and seated on a cold wet sponge at the bottom of a wheelbarrow.

While thus positioned, one of the brothers would take the initiate for a ride "on the rock road to Dublin" over the rungs of a ladder laid on the floor.

Membership in E Clampus Vitus declined in the late 1800s, but experienced a revival in the 1930s and is even stronger today. Members typically dress up in garb, usually a red miner's shirt, a black hat, and Levi's. They still hold their outrageous initiation ceremonies.

In Virginia City, there is the Julia C. Bulette Chapter No. 1864. Never mind that Miss Bulette was only the most noted prostitute in all of Virginia City. The ever-thoughtful Clampers think that all accomplishments should be acknowledged, even those of the likes of Miss Bulette, who had great compassion for the downtrodden.

There is a **Julia C. Bulette Red Light Museum** complete with photographs, dioramas, and other exhibits detailing the life of Ms. Bulette and her Virginia City brothel. Miss Bulette's favorites were said to be miners and firemen.

Miss Bulette was brutally murdered in 1867 by a thoroughgoing cad named John Millian. One hundred years later, the Julia Bulette Clampers relived that sad and stirring occasion by parading under flickering torchlight through Virginia City.

In freezing temperatures, they dedicated a state historical monument at Union and D Streets, commemorating the Comstock's old red light district that Julia called home. The Clampers, as per their custom, then dashed to the Old Washoe Club to consume a bewildering array of liquid restoratives. They then reenacted the trial and hanging of Millian for Julia's murder.

Carl Wheat, one of the founders of the revived Order of E Clampus Vitus, described the group as the "comic strip on the pages of history."

Some accounts credit a Joe Zumwalt, of Illinois, or Missouri, depending on which account you're reading, with bringing the Clamper organization to the west. Zumwalt and a Clamper brother, W.C. (or maybe C.W.) Wright was unsuccessful in opening a chapter in Hangtown (now Placerville).

After the first Chapter meeting at Mokelumne Hill in California in September 1851, Chapters began to spread throughout the gold country.

Drummers (traveling salesmen) often found it difficult to sell their wares unless they were Brothers in ECV. An early credo was "Clampers only patronize Brother Clampers."

Several fraternal organizations, such as the Masons, Elks, and Odd Fellows became prominent in the diggins'. These groups were often clannish and took their pomp and ceremony seriously.

The irreverent Clampers began cutting tin can lids into odd shapes and pinning them to their vests, mocking the fancy sashes and bejeweled vests worn by the Masons, Elks, and Odd Fellows.

Life in the diggins' was hard and entertainment virtually non-existent. The Brothers of E Clampus Vitus attempted to "lighten the load". They looked on the absurdity of life as a cherished commodity.

With tongues set firmly in cheek, they hailed each other as "Noble Grand Humbug," "Roisterous Iscutis," "Grand Imperturbable Hangman," "Clamps Vitus," and "Royal Gyascutis."

Even the name E Clampus Vitus lacks definition and is all part of the grand hoax.

The group was also a benevolent organization. Whenever a miner fell ill or died, the Clampers would collect food, money and other items for the widow.

Currently there are 40-some land-based chapters in California, Nevada, Utah and Arizona. There is as well the Floating Whang chapter, based offshore, and several outposts (incipient chapters) in Oregon and Colorado. The newest chapter arrival is CyberWhang Chapter, based in cyberspace. (Check the Internet).

115

ECV's "serious" side consists of finding, researching, and dedicating plaques to sites, incidents, and people in western history that might otherwise be overlooked. The Clampers are said to be the largest organization devoted to preserving western and mining history.

After their dedications, they traditionally have a party, known as a "doin's." This type of partying has given the Clampers a reputation as a "historical drinking society" or more correctly, "a drinking historical society".

In the old days, Clampers performed benevolent services, quietly donating food, clothing and money when disaster struck the mining camps. Thus was born this heraldic maxim: "Per Caritate Viduaribus Orphanibisque Sed Prime Viduaribus," which means, in typical Clampus lingo, that they protected widows and orphans, especially the widows.

Although they do not deny that copious amounts of "fermented, distilled, and fortified beverages" are occasionally consumed at a doin's, the group is strongly opposed to public displays of intoxication. The Clampers insist that members who imbibe have "a Brother of Sobriety holding the reins" on the ride home.

The prime requisites to becoming a Clamper are a sense of humor, an interest in western history, an open mind, and a cast iron stomach. If a man has these qualities, and strikes up a friendship with a Clamper or two, he may find himself taken in to the Ancient and Honorable Order.

But one can't simply walk up to a Clamper and ask, "Can I be a Clamper?" It is for the Brethren of ECV to invite prospective members to join. And if a man is asked, he should know that the invitation is only given once.

If the invitation is refused, it is never tendered again. As the Brethren of E Clampus Vitus maintain, Clampers are not made they're born. Like gold, they just have to be discovered.

Chapter 25

The Carson City Mint

With the opening of the Carson City Mint in 1870, the bullion from the mills could be hauled direct to Carson City, eliminating the expensive trek to San Francisco.

U.S. Mint at Carson City

The U.S. Mint at Carson City began turning out coins made with the metals of the Comstock. The mint turned out the smaller coins, along with dollars, double eagles and half eagles until 1879. It closed in 1893.

While the Carson City Mint coined gold and silver only from 1870 to 1893, it left American numismatics with a rich legacy. Most of the coins from the Carson City Mint are scarce to rare, with some being extremely rare.

Carson City silver dollars of 1882-1884 have survived in vast numbers. All of these coins, whatever their rarity or market value, carry romantic associations with the Old West and the great bonanza years of the late 19th Century.

The coins carried the letters **cc**, the only dual character mintmark among United States issues.

The Comstock Lode, discovered in 1859, was one of the richest deposits of silver ore ever found. Most of the silver ore was shipped over the Sierra Nevada Mountains to the United States Mint in San Francisco.

117

Not only were there high freight costs involved, but also there was the added problem of bandits along the way.

Mine owners petitioned Congress for a branch mint in Nevada itself. The question was put to Treasury Secretary Salmon P. Chase, who deferred the matter to Mint Director James Pollock. Pollock was an opponent of all branch mints. But the House Ways and Means Committee overruled him and a mint was approved for Nevada Territory.

The $150,000 appropriation to build the new mint fell far short of actual construction costs. Those in the east that estimated the cost based them on such a structure in the east, not for the inflated economy of the west.

It wasn't until November 1868 that the greater bulk of the mint's machinery arrived. This consisted of coin presses, blanking presses, rolling

Carson City
Mint silver dollar

mills and a variety of other implements that were shipped around the Horn.

There was an additional delay in completing the mint building itself. There was a lack of bricks in Nevada, and a chimney could not be finished until the bricks finally arrived in mid-winter.

When the dies finally arrived, the first denomination struck was the silver dollar, the symbol of Nevada's future. These dollars were of the Seated Liberty type, designed by Christian Gobrecht back in 1836 and coined in modest numbers from 1840 onward.

118

On the reverse side was a heraldic eagle with a shield upon its breast, and beneath the eagle was the Carson City mintmark, cc.

The coining of gold was begun three days later when eagles, or ten-dollar gold pieces, were minted. Unlike the silver coins which depicted the eagle with wings folded and just slightly open, the gold coins showed the eagle's wings upraised. These too carried a small cc beneath the eagle.

The Carson City mint did not produce significant numbers of coins during its first few years of operation. Nevada miners preferred to be paid for their ore with gold ingots rather than coins, which is all that was minted at Carson City. Consequently, the Nevada miners continued shipping to San Francisco.

The cost of running a mint in distant Nevada was underestimated at every stage. Virtually all of the mint's officers were members of the Republican Party. When Grover Cleveland, a Democrat, was elected president, it was seen as a real threat for the Nevada mint. The mint closed on September 11, 1885.

The mint was again funded in 1889, and the striking of coins continued. The amount of ore from Nevada mines was dropping along with the price of silver bullion. Mint Director Robert E. Preston ordered the mint closed June 1, 1893.

The Tale of the
Missing Mint Money

There was something of a scandal brewing in 1895 when a melter and refiner at the United States Mint at Carson City noticed a serious problem. Some of the ingots weighed considerably less than what they should.

The problem was reported to a supervisor and soon, a man named Andrew Mason from the New York Assay Office arrived on the scene to investigate. Mason soon learned that the Carson City Mint was short $75,550 in gold.

Included in this shortage were a small gold bar and a brick of bullion from the Standard Mine at Bodie, California. The gold brick was valued at $21,000. Under Mason's testing, it assayed at only $1,000.

Mason ordered the arrest of four persons, three of who were sent to prison. Those arrested included James Heney, a former refinery helper and silver dissolver; Henry Piper, one-time Mint employee, fired when he was found to be carrying amalgam in his lunch bucket; William Pickler, one-time policeman and a former deposit melter at the Mint; and John Jones, an assistant refiner at the Mint.

Heney was accused of taking gold to a Reno reduction works to be cast into ingots, which were valued at $23,000. He maintained that he had gotten the gold from a mine in Idaho but the prosecutor pointed out that no mine could produce gold that assayed 980 fine. The ingots had the same degree of purity as that turned out by the Carson City Mint.

William Pickler died before he came to trial, but not before a cache of gold and silver amalgam was unearthed beneath a manure pile in his barnyard. Some mystery surrounded his death since he was only 34 years old. Some believed he had been poisoned to prevent his testimony. Others claimed it was suicide.

Henry Piper was fined $300. He escaped going to prison because it was felt he was only lax in reporting his suspicions to his employers.

John Jones was sentenced to eight years in prison, but served only six.

Resources
1. "Nevada, Official Bicentennial Book," Edited by Stanley W. Paher
2. "History of Nevada." By Russell R. Elliott
3. "Touring Nevada," by Mary Ellen and Al Glass

Chapter 26

Hooper's fantastic turkey drive

Henry Hooker owned a hardware business in Hangtown (now Placerville, California). He considered selling merchandise to gold miners as more lucrative than prospecting for gold himself.

His business was indeed bustling until a fire destroyed a great deal of the town, including Henry's store. He was left with $1,000 to his name.

But Henry was also a forward thinking trader ever looking for a new opportunity. He knew that about all gold rush miners ate were some beef, but mostly beans and bacon.

Hooker decided he would provide the miners with something better. He decided to drive a flock of turkeys to Carson City. Turkeys were plentiful on the local ranches around Placerville, but scarce in Nevada.

Henry was sure that a turkey drive over the Sierra Nevada could be a successful financial venture. He was sure he could sell the gobblers for a luxury price.

Hooker then went on a buying spree, paying $1.50 each to the Placerville ranchers for the turkeys. He did have to put up with a lot of smart-alecky and snide remarks concerning his plans.

Finally, his flock grew to 500 birds. Henry was out of pocket $750 for the lot. He kept the rest of his bankroll to hire a helper, buy two dogs to help herd the birds, and to buy provisions.

From Hangtown to Carson City lay a distance of sixty plus miles of mountain country. Compared to other livestock, herding turkeys is slow motion. Hooker's herd dogs hardly panted from their exercise and the horse Henry was riding even put on weight during the slow journey.

Portions of the area between Hangtown and Carson City were covered with snow. The resourceful Hooker walked his turkeys through warm tar and then sand to give them extra protection in the snow.

The turkeys decided when it was time to stop for the night. They roosted on the ground at night, and Henry stopped whenever they decided to rest.

Henry herded the birds over the crest of the Sierra without incident. They continued down the slope toward Carson City. The birds milled along the edge of a deep and rugged slope.

The barking dogs pressed the birds but they refused to negotiate the slope. Suddenly, the birds stampeded. They spread their wings, flew over the precipice and raced away. Hooker could only watch his investment disappear into the dense brush below.

Hooker later said, "I had the most indescribable feeling of my whole life. I thought here it is–goodbye turkeys! My finances were at low ebb; these turkeys were my whole earthly possession. I thought of my wife and children who were expecting me back with the profits from my venture, all of which appeared to have gone glimmering in a few minutes."

Fortune was on Henry's side. As soon as the turkeys landed, they began gobbling and calling to each other. They then reassembled themselves. Hooker and his dogs were able to locate the flock and drive them on toward Carson City.

When he arrived with the birds, Hooker was able to sell each one of them for five dollars each. Soon after returning to Hangtown, he moved his family to Arizona, and with the proceeds from his turkey drive, launched a ranching business.

He eventually accumulated property that measured thirty miles long and twenty-seven miles wide. He named the ranch Sierra Bonita.

Resources

1. Nevada, Official Bicentennial Book, edited by Stanley W. Paher.
2. Numerous versions of this story have been printed and reprinted over the years and it is difficult if not impossible to find original sources.

Chapter 27

Aurora: *as wild and wooly as they come*

Before the boundary line was surveyed, Aurora, Nevada, was
the county seat of Mono County, California.

(Westerner's Brand Book, No. 11)

In 1864, a roaring dispute arose between the Pond and the
Real del Monte mining companies. Both claimed to have rights
to the same ore ledge, from opposite ends.

While awaiting a court to settle the argument, both
companies hired gunman to enforce their right to continue
mining and to protect their claim from claim jumpers.

The litigation between the two companies dragged on for
months. During the waiting for a court decision, a man by the
name of Jimmy Sears stole a horse. W.R. Johnson sent one of
his employees to catch Sears and bring back the horse. The
employee, in what he considered his line of duty, shot and killed
Sears.

The gunmen from both sides considered themselves
employees of one or the other of the mining companies. The

killing was blamed on Johnson, who had ordered his employee to chase down Sears, and not on the employee who had committed the shooting.

Mark Twain stayed in this cabin with Bob Howland and Horatio (Raish) Phillips. The cabin measured ten feet by twelve feet and was located near the Chinese section of town. (Nevada Historical Society)

While the lawsuit dragged on over the ore ledge, the gunmen from both companies became well ensconced in Aurora. When the suit finally came to an end nine months later, the gunslingers continued their residency in Aurora, a fact that disturbed many townspeople.

A problem was that law enforcement officers had been urged by wealthy mine owners to ignore the gunman during the dispute and now it was too late for the lawmen to gain the upper hand.

One group of the outlaw toughs decided they would avenge the death of their friend Sears who had been killed for stealing a horse. The gunmen killed Johnson, the employer, and attempted to burn his body in the street.

This brought a call for action from the Aurora townspeople. Aurora lawmen then began tracking the outlaws that had murdered Johnson.

A vigilance committee called "601" was formed. Territorial Governor James Nye was alerted to a planned hanging of four miscreants from a single gallows for the murder of Johnson without benefit of a trial.

Nye wired Samuel Youngs, Aurora's representative to the 1861 territorial legislature, to keep order. Youngs wired back that all was quiet and orderly; that four men would be hanged in one half hour.

Governor Nye came to Aurora, saw the gallows and inquired as to what it was. Some quick thinker told him it was a "hay press" which apparently satisfied his curiosity. The town did become more quiet and peaceful after the hanging.

Aurora had a population of 10,000 people. It produced at last thirty million in bullion over a ten-year period. J.M. Corey, one of the prospectors who discovered gold there, named Aurora for the Goddess of Dawn.

The citizens of Aurora were never quite sure whether they lived in Nevada or California. Mono County was created by the California legislature on Mary 24, 1861, and Aurora was made the county seat.

When the Nevada territorial government met on November 25,1861, it too, selected Aurora as the county seat for Esmeralda County, Nevada.

Aurora citizens came up with a novel plan to resolve the problem as Election Day 1863 neared. Each county put up a full slate of officers and voters cast two sets of ballots, one at the Armory Hall for Esmeralda candidates, and one at the police station for Mono County nominees.

Holt's 1863 map shows the rich Esmeralda mines of Aurora to be in California. Nevada and California vied for political control of that area until a survey late in 1863 placed Aurora in Nevada.

This solution meant that no matter what decision the survey party made, both counties would have officers without needing a special election. On September 22, it was determined that Aurora was indeed in Nevada. Bridgeport then became the county seat for Mono County.

Little is left of Aurora today, mainly because scavengers looting bricks from the town and reportedly selling them in Reno for sixty-five dollars per thousand have destroyed it.

In Aurora in 1863, hay cost $1.25 per day to keep a horse in a stable. Eggs were $1.50 a dozen. One old mountaineer gathered duck and gull eggs on the cinder-cone islands of Mono Lake and sold them for a tidy profit.

Only metallic money was in evidence. People were hostile to paper.

Resources

1. ”Desert Challenge,” by Richard G. Lillard
2. “Ghost Towns and Mining Camps of California,” By Remi Nadeau.
3. “Nevada Official Bicentennial Book,” edited by Stanley Paher.

A desert prospector tests his ore samples.   (Farm Security Aministration)

Chapter 28

Austin's famous sack of flour

How much credence can be put in the story that a horse discovered the town of Austin, Nevada is unsure, but whatever the story, Austin must have been one dusty town.

State Senator M.J. Farrell once described a "bath" in Austin as "consisting of two inches of cold water in a big tub, a piece of brown soap, a napkin, and a dollar and a half."

The editor of the Austin *Reveille* was likewise unkind. He said Austin's communication with the outside world was carried on by means of "mud wagons," called stages for the sake of courtesy.

Reuel C. Gridley and his sack of flour.
(Nevada Historical Society)

Austin's history ties in with the Overland Stage and the Pony Express. William Talcott was the keeper of the Jacob Springs stage station. In 1862, Talcott found ore in Pony Canyon and had it assayed. It proved to be rich in silver.

The high walls around Austin are pockmarked with abandoned prospect holes. Austin was the mother town of central and eastern Nevada mining. It was from this base that Tuscarora, Eureka, Hamilton, and several other camps were discovered.

One of the exciting events of Austin's early years was the arrival of nine camels, including one that had been presented to the U.S. Government by the Sultan of Turkey.

Jefferson Davis, as Secretary of War, was interested in the animals as beasts of burden on the deserts of the Southwest. While the experiment was deemed successful, it lost support when Davis left office to become President of the Confederacy.

Austin's biggest claim to fame may have had to do with a sack of flour. Grocer Reuel Colt Gridley, a Missouri Democrat, made a bet with Dr. H.S. Herrick, a Republican, on the outcome of a local election.

If the Republicans won, Herrick was to carry a 50-pound sack of flour from Upper Austin to Clifton; if the Democrats won, Gridley would do the opposite. Gridley lost the bet and carried the flower to the Bank Exchange in Austin.

There it was decided that the sack of flour should be auctioned off with the proceeds going to the Sanitary Fund, an organization set up to care for the sick and wounded in the Union armies.

At the auction, the sack of flour brought a mere five dollars. This wasn't considered acceptable so the group held a second auction. The bidding, this time, was high and wild, and each purchaser donated the sack of flour back to the Sanitary Fund. The final result was the sack of flour auction brought in about $3,000.

The next day, another auction was held. This time, $1,700 was received. Gridley like the auction idea, so he carried it to Virginia City where he raked in $8,000. In Sacramento, he netted another $10,000, and in San Francisco, he collected $15,000.

When Gridley had finished trudging around with his sack of flour, he had collected close to $100,000 for the Sanitary Fund.

Another story of Austin is the appointment, in 1919, of a woman to the job of sheriff. Clara Dunham Crowell was married to George Crowell, who was elected to the sheriff's job. When he died in office, city fathers appointed Clara to the job.

They pointedly told her that the job was in name only, and that her deputy was to do all the necessary "strong-arm" stuff.

134

This did not sit well with Clara. "If I am to be appointed," she said, "then I will be sheriff."

Clara not only went to the office each day, overseeing all of the duties of the sheriff position, but she even entered the fray of what could have been a dangerous situation. She was told of a fight that was brewing in a saloon.

She went to the saloon, despite the fact that it was unheard of for a woman of good reputation to enter such an establishment, to arrest the two individuals. She arrested both men and took them to jail.

When Clara heard of a case where whiskey was being sold to an Indian, which was against the law, she devised a plan to catch the culprit.

Clara Crowell, Lander
County Sheriff

The Indian in this case was Grant Williamson, the son of "Old Topsy," a favorite of Austin housewives for whom she worked. Topsy was a devoted mother and often followed her son around to protect him.

A meeting was arranged between the Indian and the guilty saloonkeeper. Clara disguised herself as "Topsy" and stationed herself near the rendezvous where the whiskey would be traded. When the saloonkeeper handed over the whiskey, Clara suddenly appeared, throwing back her coat to reveal her badge.

Resources
1. "Nevada, Official Bicentennial Book," Edited by Stanley Paher.
2. "Ghost Towns of Nevada," by Donald C. Miller
3. "Touring Nevada," by Mary Ellen and Al Glass

4. "Nevada, A Guide to the Silver State," Compiled by Writers' Program of Works Project Administration.

Chapter 29

Boulder Canyon Project:
One of man's great feats

Hoover Dam and Lake Mead

Hoover Dam and Lake Mead collect the waters of several major rivers, including the Gunnison River in Colorado, the Green and San Juan Rivers in Utah, the Little Colorado and Gila Rivers in Arizona, and the Virgin River in Nevada.

One of the most difficult steps in gaining approval for the Boulder Canyon Project was determining the equitable allocation of the waters of the Colorado River. The people living in the Colorado River Basin depended on the waters from the river. In many cases, water rights had even greater value than land titles.

There was a concern about one state's ability to claim the lion's share of the water, leaving another state without sufficient

137

water for development. Under water rights law, an individual or agency meeting certain legal conditions and first appropriating water for beneficial use had first right to the water.

It was feared that California, with its vast financial resources would be the first state to begin beneficial use and therefore claim rights to the majority of the water from the Colorado. The parties involved recognized that some sort of agreement on water distribution was need or the project could not proceed.

A commission was formed with a representative from each of the Basin states and one from the Federal Government. The Government's representative was Herbert Hoover, then Secretary of Commerce under President Harding. The Commission first met in January 1922.

When the commission attempted to establish amounts for each state, agreement could not be reached. Hoover, who presided over the commission, suggested another approach. This would be to divide the water from the Colorado into two groups, the Upper and the Lower Basin States, with the division of water within each Basin to be agreed upon at a later date.

The proposal, called the Hoover Compromise, led to the Colorado River Compact. The Legislatures in six basin states and the Federal Government approved the compact.

The Boulder Canyon Project Act was approved on December 21, 1928. The site of the dam is a deep canyon more than 30 miles from the nearest town. Provisions had to be made to haul the nearly 5,000 workmen to the project.

To house the estimated 5,000 workers and officials involved with the project, the Government designed and built Boulder City. The site for this city is about six miles west of the dam. It was selected because it was at a higher elevation than the surrounding countryside.

Accidents and injuries were expected on a project the size of Boulder Dam. One of the most notable accidents did occur during tunnel lining operations. Three men had just finished loosening a section of the form in the tunnel invert when a cable hoisting the form upward to the next section gave way.

The form, with the three men still standing on it, plummeted down the inclined shaft towards the Colorado River flowing through the diversion tunnel below. The remaining workers heard a tremendous splash in the water below.

One of them telephoned a warning to workers downstream from the tunnel portals. A rescue team was ready when the form, with the men still clinging to it, emerged from the tunnel. The men were battered and beaten, but somehow had survived their quarter-mile ride through the tunnels of Boulder Dam.

One of the more memorable characters involved in the construction of Boulder Dam was a black dog named "Nig". He was a black Labrador mix and was born under the floor of the first police building in Boulder City.

Nig had free reign to go anywhere he wanted. Each morning he would ride to the dam in the company transport. At night he was always ready to head back to town with the other workers. In the mess hall, he was given anything he wanted. In the mornings, workers would pack him a lunch and he would eat with them at noon.

In the evenings, he would hang out at the drug store in Boulder City where workers would buy him ice cream and candy. Once he got sick from all the sweets. He was taken to the town doctor. The doctor placed an ad in the local paper, saying, "Please do not feed me ice cream and candy bars. It makes me sick." It was signed "Nig". It worked. Workers were then more careful what they gave the dog.

Nig liked to ride on the equipment at the dam. He could be seen riding on one of the trains or on one of the skips that carried men up and down the side of the canyon. Sometimes he would ride around the construction site with Frank Crowe, superintendent for the Six Companies firm helping to build the dam.

One hot summer day, Nig was asleep in the shade under a truck. The driver didn't see him and Nig didn't hear the truck

139

start. The truck ran over him. He was buried near the dam and the workers took up a collection for a plaque, which was placed on the canyon wall.

Years later, a visitor to the dam saw the plaque and complained that the name "Nig" was racist, and began a campaign to have the plaque removed. In 1979, the Bureau of Reclamation did remove the plaque.

The citizens of Boulder City began a petition drive protesting the removal. One worker on the project noted, "Nig was all he was ever known by. He was the friend of both the black men and the white men and every other kind of person that worked down there."

The plaque was replaced with a new plaque. This one did not have Nig's name on it, but it did have his picture on it. The workmen pouring the concrete for the new plaque took care of that matter. They scratched "Nig" in the concrete. It is still there.

Resources

1. "The Boulder Canyon Project," by William Joe Simonds.
2. There is a host of bibliographical material available at the website: www.nevada-history.org. This excellent web site is particularly valuable in that it has two serious historians connected with it making the material quite dependable.

Chapter 30

Goldfield's famous prize fight

The Nelson-Ganz fight at Goldfield
(Nevada Historical Society)

By 1906, the silver mines in Goldfield had pretty much played out. Prospectors were moving on. To say it was hurting the business of George 'Tex" Rickard's Northern Saloon was a giant understatement.

Rickard used Goldfield as kind of a stopover in his varied activities. He had worked as a cowpuncher, a marshal, a miner, and gambler in places ranging from Texas to the Yukon and Alaska.

Tex Rickard and his Northern Saloon may have been a little down, but not out. Tex knew just what he and the town needed to revive business. Goldfield needed a PRIZE fight.

Goldfield, you see, wasn't just any little mining camp in Nevada. Goldfield produced more gold in the first year of its existence than was produced by any other camp in the same time. One Goldfield booster cried, "It will surpass the Comstock."

Goldfield, Nevada, in 1906   (Nevada Historical Society)

Goldfield was known for its "jewelry ore" and people were sure the town would bounce back when miners would unlock new deposits. Residents refused to sell their homes when they could still make a profit, hanging on for the town's second coming.

Tex Rickard got financing for a world's lightweight championship of the world bout for Goldfield. The fight would feature Oscar "Battling" Nelson, the "Durable Dane", against black challenger Joe Gans.

The fight attracted fans and gamblers from all parts of the country. The Tonopah & Goldfield Railroad put in sidetracks for the 300 Pullman cars expected to arrive for the fight. The battle was scheduled for Labor Day, 1906.

An estimated 7,000 people paid about $70,000 to see the fight. Goldfield saloons closed all day. It was a history-making day in Goldfield, the only time in history that many would see such an event.

Nelson was a rough-and-tumble fighter who lacked science but hit hard. He was aggressive and won many bouts due to his remarkable stamina. According to many historians Nelson was defending the lightweight championship against Gans.

However, other news accounts of the time recognized the bout as Gans defending his title. Gans fought Joe Walcott to a draw in 1904 for the welterweight championship. The press continued to recognize Gans as the rightful lightweight champion and since there were no commissions he should be clearly recognized as the true titleholder.

The fight lasted 42 rounds with Joe Gans being declared the winner when Nelson fouled Gans in a clinch. Gans won $10,000 for the fight, but Tex Rickard's fight had brought a gate total of some $72,000. Rickard eventually made it to New York City and the Madison Square Gardens.

Goldfield was an ideal location, one of the great mining camps of all time. The purse was $33,500, of which Gans was to receive $11,000 and Nelson $22,500. The gate receipt was $76,000 the largest ever realized for a prizefight in America up to that time. The official attendance was 6,200. The odds at ringside were 2-1 Gans.

As much as the Gans-Nelson fight built up Goldfield, fire and flood destroyed the town. In 1923, a fire consumed fifty-three blocks in the center of town. In 1932, two cloudbursts sent torrents of water swirling into town and washed away many buildings.

Tex Rickard sensed that Goldfield had met its demise. He put a sign on the church, proclaiming, "This church is closed. God has gone to Rawhide."

Resources

1. "Desert Challenge," by Richard G. Lillard
2. "Ghost Towns of Nevada," by Donald C. Miller
3. "Saloons of Nevada," By Raymond M. Smith
4. "Nevada, A Guide to the Silver State," compiled by the Writers' Program of the Works Project Administration.
5. "It Happened in Nevada," by Elizabeth Gibson

Chapter 31

The hanging of Elizabeth Potts

This is the gallows, shown being built and numbered in Placerville, California for shipment to Elko, Nevada. Elizabeth and Josiah Potts were hung from the structure.

(Nevada Historical Society)

It was a dual hanging, but it marked the first and only time a woman was executed in Nevada.

Both Elizabeth Potts and her husband, Josiah, were convicted of the same murder. Josiah accompanied his wife up the scaffold from which they were hanged. Charles Sproule, editor of the Elko Free Press wrote, "She was the leader, he was the tool."

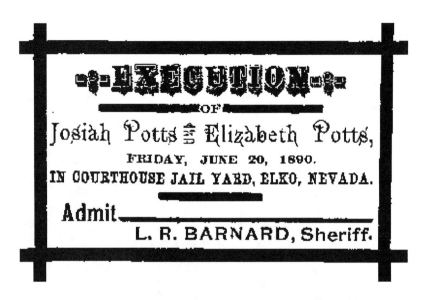

Invitation to the Potts Hangings (Nevada Historical Society)

The murder happened in Carlin, Nevada, a young but active railroad town, 23 miles west of Elko and situated along Interstate 80.

Elizabeth and Josiah Potts lived in a small cabin just outside Carlin with their sixteen-year-old son, Charles, and four-year-old daughter Edith. Potts was employed as a machinist at the Southern Pacific Railroad shops.

Miles Faucett, an old man that had become wealthy by horse-trading, was a frequent visitor at the Potts' home. Mrs. Potts did his laundry and cooked for him. Neighbors last saw him when he hitched his team of horses in front of the Potts' home.

Josiah Potts told curious neighbors that Faucett had sold him the team before leaving for California. He was able to produce a bill-of-sale to prove his point. The Potts family soon moved to Rock Springs, Wyoming.

The investigation into the murder of Miles Faucett actually began after George Brewer and his wife had moved into the Potts vacant cabin. They kept hearing eerie noises during the night. George, carrying an iron rod for protection, went into the cellar of the house to investigate.

146

He found a soft spot in the ground that indicated someone had dug up the floor. Brewer poked his rod into the ground but failed to find anything peculiar.

A week later, he went into the cellar again. "I saw something that looked like a rotten turnip," he told police. "I pulled up some hair and the smell came with it." Brewer immediately contacted Deputy George McIntosh, who in turn telegraphed Sheriff Lou Barnard in Elko.

When the officers dug into the soft floor, they unearthed the mutilated remains of a man. The body had been cut into several pieces. Brewer told the Elko Free Press, "The head looked as though it was cut off right straight across below the ears."

The burned and decayed remains were unidentifiable. But an old knife discovered in one the dead man's pockets were recognized as having belonged to Miles Faucett.

Josiah and Elizabeth Potts migrated from Manchester, England, to the U.S. in 1865. The couple produced seven children, but for reasons unknown, most were adopted into different families in several states. With them were only Charles and Edith.

The murder victim also came from Manchester, England, and became a friend of the Potts family. He was invited to spend New Year's Day, 1887, with them. It was the last time he was seen alive.

After District Attorney W.C. Love presented his sparse but damaging evidence to the Elko Grand Jury. Elizabeth was calm and in control when she was called to the witness stand.

She claimed that her husband was searching in a trunk for a stamp to send for a catalog when he came across a letter Elizabeth had written to Deputy McIntosh but never mailed. In the letter, she recounted how Faucett had lived in the Potts' barn while he was mining and before he moved to a ranch property he later purchased.

One afternoon she noticed her daughter Edith was missing. While searching for the child, she found Faucett in the barn sitting on the edge of his bed in his drawers. Edith was sitting astride his legs with her drawers unbuttoned.

"You old wretch," she shrieked. "I'll have you tarred and feathered for that at least." She told the jury that Faucett then grabbed her by the neck and choked her, and then made her promise not to tell what happened.

"By the way he looked, he would kill me if I did not," said Elizabeth. "So, I kept doing his baking and washing as usual but kept brooding over it all the time. I didn't tell Josiah."

She claimed what she did do was write an account of the episode, intending to mail it to Deputy McIntosh. When Josiah found the letter, he was enraged. He confronted Faucett, and Faucett dropped to his knees, screaming that he didn't know what he was doing.

Faucett offered to give the Potts everything he owned in payment of a $180 debt. Elizabeth composed a bill of sale, which Faucett signed.

Reaching with his left hand, Faucett grabbed a revolver off a shelf, saying, "You folks will be blamed for this." He then fired and sank to the floor.

Josiah said he sent his wife and son to bed while he contemplated what to do with the body. He wrapped Faucett's body in blankets and carried it to the cellar, where he buried it. After three months had passed, Josiah said he became worried the body would be discovered.

He dug up the cadaver, cut it into small pieces, and tried to burn it. He had to give up the task because of the smell, he said. He then reburied the body pieces.

It took the jury about four hours to return a verdict. Elizabeth and Josiah were indicted for killing Faucett. On March 22, the courtroom was crowded to overflowing. The judge sentenced them "to be hanged by the neck until dead."

Resources

1. Nevada Official Bicentennial Book

2. Web site: www.rabbitbrush.com/hickson/potts.html
3. Nevada State Archives

Chapter 32

The 'long tongue' of the west

Indians called the Overland Telegraph the "long tongue." The Overland Telegraph contributed to the quick demise of the Pony Express and was considered one of the greatest achievements of the nineteenth century.

Samuel Morse put the first American telegraph line into operation in the spring of 1844, and by December 1847, the wires had reached St. Louis. A cable had been laid across the Atlantic before the telegraph was ready to tackle the west.

On June 16, 1860, about ten weeks after the Pony Express began operations, Congress authorized a bill that would spell the end of it. This bill instructed the Secretary of the Treasury to subsidize the building of a transcontinental telegraph line to connect the Missouri River and the Pacific Coast.

While the lines were under construction the Pony Express operated as usual. Letters and newspapers were carried the entire length of the line from St. Joseph to Sacramento.

The California State Telegraph Company ran a line from Fort Churchill, a U.S. Army fort built in 1861 to provide protection for early settlers, to Salt Lake City. The company placed twenty-five to thirty poles every mile for the entire distance of 570 miles.

They didn't anticipate what happened next. Almost immediately, the Texas woodpecker went to work riddling the poles, probably to get at insects that had invaded the lumber. There were other problems as well. The construction gangs battled against alkali, soft shifting sand, solid rock, and a lack of drinking water and animal feed.

In October, a message was sent over the line from San Francisco to St. Joseph, Missouri. Westerners called it "the great achievement of the nineteenth century."

An office or repair station was required every thirty to fifty miles along the line to keep things operating. Rains and floods loosened the poles. Brush fires burned them down. Lightning not only knocked poles down but burned the instruments. In marshes and sinks of mushy alkali, fallen wires shorted.

Things were even worse in the Sierra. Falling timbers, avalanches, sleet, washouts in the spring, and forest fires in summer raised havoc with the telegraph lines. In a severe storm there might be as many as thirty breaks in a hundred miles.

When the telegraph wires could not be connected, men on horseback carried dispatches from the two last stations on either side of the gap. One San Francisco resident wired a friend in Virginia City and received a reply in six hours.

He was incensed. He felt he should have gotten his answer four hours earlier. He wasn't aware that his message had passed through a dozen breaks in the line, was carried over several gaps by mounted men, and transported through floods and snowstorms.

On October 26 the wires were joined, and San Francisco was in direct contact with New York City. On that day the Pony Express was officially terminated, but it was not until November that the last letters completed their journey over the route.

Sources

1. "The Story of the Pony Express," By Waddell Smith
2. "Desert Challenge," By Richard G. Lillard
3. "The Humboldt," By Dale L. Morgan

Chapter 33

Virginia City: richest city in the west

The main street in Virginia City.

No town in the west caused the sensation that Virginia City did with the finding of the rich Comstock Lode. Its mines were the richest yet discovered in the United States, including California, where the gold rush began.

As miners continued finding more and more ore, Virginia City became the city in which to make one's fortune. The history of Virginia City is, to a very considerable degree, the history of Nevada.

The story of Virginia City began when two miners, Ethan Allen Grosch and Hosea Ballou Grosch found rich ore deposits in what was called Gold Canyon. They died under tragic circumstances before their claims were recorded.

Henry T. P. Comstock, known as Old Pancake, was a sheepherder and an inept prospector who took possession of the brothers' cabin and tried to find their old sites. Comstock was described as someone who knew little but claimed a lot. He would stick his nose into everything. He was a blowfly buzzing up and down and across the new diggings.

Henry Comstock one day stumbled upon Pat McLaughlin and Peter O'Reilly who discovered a gold-bearing quartz ledge at the head of Six Mile Canyon in 1859. When Comstock noticed what appeared to be rich ore on the edge of the hole in which the two Irishmen were working, he immediately told them he had made a prior filing on the site.

McLaughlin and O'Reilly accepted Comstock's story as being true and allowed him into the deal. As the word got out, pick and shovel men soon dotted the hillside. Virginia City's lots, with preferred frontage, soared to $10,000 to $20,000 each.

One author said, "It is one of the pleasant ironies to which the West is heir that the greatest treasure hill ever known should bear the name of a loud-mouthed sheepherder."

The ore was dirty and hard to process. After crushing and panning the ore for gold, the discolored remains were quickly thrown away. It wasn't until a prospector who was familiar with silver took some of the ore and had it assayed that the truth was found. The discarded waste the miners had tossed aside assayed at over $4,000 per ton in silver—more than the value per ton of gold already extracted.

Virginia City got its name when a drunken miner known as "Old Virginny" was stumbling toward his shack one evening carrying a bottle of whiskey. He fell and the booze smashed against a rock. Old Virginny shouted to his comrades, "I baptize this spot Virginny Town." His comrades, as miners were wont to do, adjourned to the bars to celebrate the newly dignified town.

When the town really boomed with its newfound silver ore, Virginny Town became Virginia City, and was the most important settlement between Denver and San Francisco.

With the riches pouring forth from the bowels of Mount Davidson, grubby prospectors were made into instant millionaires. They built lavish mansions, imported furniture and fashions from Europe and the Orient, and financed the Civil War.

At its peak, Virginia City was a boisterous town with something going on 24 hours a day, both above and below ground. A minister in Virginia City marveled at the vigilantes' "dreadful government" as being so secretive, brutal, and controlling, but at the same time cited a "most perfect acquiescence" and his own gratefulness for the "existence of such a Committee."

Vigilante justice thrust violent retribution into everyday lives that courts did not. A gold town resident might stroll down a street or venture into a nearby gulch and find blue-faced men hanging from trees, windlasses, roof beams or corral bars."

Walking home from school in Virginia City in1864, young Mollie Sheehan came upon a vigilante hanging in an unfinished building. "The air was charged with excitement. The bodies of five men with ropes around their necks hung limp from a roof beam."

Virginia City had two disastrous fires. Each time the town rebuilt even finer than before.

Resources

1. "Precious Dust," by Paula Mitchell Marks
2. "Helldorados, Ghosts and Camps of the old Southwest," by Norman D. Weis
3. "The Humboldt, High Road of the West," by Dale L. Morgan
4. "Desert Challenge," by Richard G. Lillard

Chapter 34

Treasure Hill and its big boom

A.J. Leathers, a blacksmith, had an Indian friend named Napias Jim. Jim showed Leathers a piece of rich ore from which the blacksmith produced a button of silver.

The price of the white metal then was $1.32 an ounce. The location of the ore that Napias Jim showed Leathers became the Hidden Treasure Mine. The ore assayed from five hundred to eight hundred dollars a ton.

Other mining companies moved in and by the spring of 1868 Nevada's shortest, most intense mining rush began. Treasure Hill was a magnet for every boomer, promoter, card shark, merchant-capitalist, prostitute and prospector in the west.

Hamilton and Treasure City both became short time boomtowns. Hamilton became a promoters dream with residential lots selling for a flat $5,000. A corner lot on Main Street was sold for $25,000.

Treasure City was originally named *Tesora* and a post office with that name opened on April 23, 1869. On Jun 15, 1869 the name was officially changed to Treasure City. It gained a reputation for its "mail races."

Wells Fargo had an office in Treasure City and another three miles down the slope of Treasure Hill at the town of Hamilton. Each day the stage brought mail to Hamilton. Mounted riders would grab the mail sacks of rival express companies and then race up the three-mile stretch carrying mail to Treasure City.

Bets were placed daily on which rider would win. Claims, mines and entire fortunes were wagered on the mail races.

Silver was discovered high up on the east side of Treasure Hill in 1867. This discovery went on to become the famous Hidden Treasure Mine.

Within a year, over 6000 people called Treasure City home. There were more than 13,000 claims filed on Treasure hill. The silver mines were so rich they threatened to glut the world money market. The British were said to be heavy investors in the area.

Treasure City, where the citizens would place bets on riders carrying the mail.

There were open mine shafts everywhere on Treasure Hill. In some places the main street through town had to make a quick jog to miss a mineshaft. In the center of town, a rock wall was built to hold mine waste from rolling down on the main street.

Life was pretty rough here, at an altitude of over 9000 feet. The town took the brunt of icy winds that howled through the streets. Deep snowdrifts would destroy buildings and block the roads.

At the town's peak in 1869, Treasure City had a newspaper, "White Pine News", post office, stock exchange, theater, and Odd Fellows Lodges. The business district had at least 42 stores, a bank, Wells Fargo Office, and several saloons.

Treasure City's main thoroughfare jogs to miss open mine shafts.
(Photo taken by Norman D. Weis)

Like so many other boomtowns, Treasure City soon found that its mines contained only deposits, and not large veins of ore.

Resources

1. "Helldorados, Ghosts and Camps of the Old Southwest," by Norman D. Weis.
2. "Desert Challenge," by Richard G. Lillard
3. "Touring Nevada," by Mary Ellen and Al Glass

Chapter 35

The Sutro Tunnel, too late to do its job

The Sutro Tunnel is called an engineering marvel even though it was finished too late to do its job. That job was to drain water from the deep mines, where hot water temperatures reached unbearable levels, through a four-mile tunnel and, at the same time, provide transportation for the ore.

The mucker train with mules used to remove material dug from the four-mile trace of the Sutro Tunnel.

(Special Collections Library, University of Nevada, Reno)

This grand engineering project was the plan of Adolph Sutro, who not only had an unusual knowledge of civil engineering, but was a master in dealing with bankers, legislators, and his enemies on the Lode, who did everything they could to thwart him.

Sutro was operating a cigar store in Virginia City when he conceived the tunnel idea. The legislature of the new State of Nevada passed a bill incorporating the tunnel company on February 4, 1865. The following year, an act of Congress chartered the corporation.

To finance his plan, Sutro contracted with 19 mining companies for a royalty payment of two-dollars a ton on all the ore removed through the tunnel. He promised to drain the water from the mines free, saving the companies enormous pumping costs.

Adolph Sutro (left) and party at the Sutro tunnel.
(Nevada Historical Society)

The Sutro Tunnel Company was given a charter to sink mining shafts along the line as long as they did not infringe on the rights of miners with previous claims.

Sutro didn't get financing for the tunnel until 1868, the year a disastrous fire deep in the Yellow Jacket Mine killed hundreds of miners. Sutro's Tunnel would have saved many lives. After that disaster, Sutro obtained a pledge for $50,000 from the Virginia and Gold Hill miners' unions and started work on the tunnel in 1869.

Sutro encountered a lot of problems in raising money for the project. The sale of stock in Sutro Tunnel Company finally enabled construction to begin in 1869. Sutro was eventually forced to turn to England for financing. He obtained major financing from the banking house of McCalmont Brothers and Company.

Nearly nine years after the initial groundbreaking, the tunnel was completed. The tunnel stretched 20,484 feet from the mouth to the first connection with the lode at the 1,650-foot level of the Savage mine. The cost of construction was approximately three and one-half million dollars. In 1880, two billion gallons of water were pumped from the mines through the tunnel.

The town of Sutro sprang up in 1872 between the mouth of the tunnel and the Carson River. Adolph Sutro had a mansion built—a colossal $40,000 white Victorian structure connected by iron cables to the hardrock in Sun Mountain (Mount Davidson).

Sutro wanted assurance that his home wouldn't be damaged by the high winds called "Washoe zephyrs." Sutro hoped that a pond near his home could be used to raise frogs, but the plan came to naught.

Blacksmith shops, foundries, machine shops, a church, a hotel, five saloons, a dance hall, a newspaper, a hospital, and other buildings were erected to accommodate the workers and the building process of the Sutro Tunnel.

Some 3 00 t o 4 00 m en worked eight-hour s hifts t o p unch t he t unnel through the mountain. Sutro wanted to design the town in a gridiron pattern. There would be fifty streets running east and west. Avenues running north to south would be named for women from Adele through Zeline.

Mine owners refused to pay the $2 per ton fee they had contracted to pay the Sutro Tunnel Company to haul ore out on the underground railway. This affected the tunnel's profitability. The Sutro Tunnel continued draining the mines until 1940.

Sutro was a Prussian immigrant who was only 30 years old when he first visited the Comstock in 1860. He went to the Comstock for the express purpose of opening a merchandise store similar to one he owned in San Francisco.

He sold his store in San Francisco and built a small stamp mill in Dayton, Nevada in 1861. It may be here that he conceived the idea for a tunnel. Sutro made almost daily trips by horseback through Six-Mile Canyon to the ore bodies in the lode. His stamp mill was destroyed by fire in 1863, which freed Sutro for the Tunnel project, a task that would keep him busy for the next fifteen years.

Sutro ran into serious opposition from the banking crowd on the Comstock. They felt he was trying to gain control of the Comstock.

The mine was completed too late to help the Comstock Lode. It had already begun its decline and the fall was never reversed.

Adolph Sutro sold out his interest in the tunnel company in 1878 and moved to San Francisco. He died a millionaire in 1898. He had taken his meager returns from the Tunnel and invested in San Francisco real estate at depression prices in 1879.

Resources

1. "Touring Nevada," by Mary Ellen and Al Glass
2. "Nevada, A Guide to the Silver State," compiled by the Writers' Program of the Work Projects Administration
3. "History of Nevada," by Russell R. Elliott
4. "Ghost Towns of Nevada," by Donald C. Miller

Chapter 36

Nevada saloons had their place

There was probably nothing that played a more important role in the miner's leisure hours than the mining camp saloons.

They sprang up as soon as a new strike was announced. The crude affairs often served as bar, hotel, general store, restaurant, post office and barbershop.

The liquor served in these thrown-up-overnight establishments could be potent enough to kill or make you wish it had. Most of the alcohol served in the mining camp saloons was nothing more than cheap alcohol mixed with anything that might give it flavor and color. Burnt sugar, cheap rum, or even tobacco might be used to gain the desired effect.

Drinks sported colorful names. The Shawn O'Farrell was a glass of whiskey with a beer chaser. (Whiskey was meant to cut the dust and the beer to quench the thirst.) A miner might order other colorful drinks, such as Red Eye, Rattlesnake Juice, Forty Rod, Taos Lightening, Hemlock Brandy, White Mule and Panther Piss.

The bar often held bottles of Old Crow and Golden Wedding and other famous brands, all filled from the same keg of green whiskey.

Bars and gaming tables sprang up in impromptu buildings. It was no accident that the early westerner fell into the habit of bragging about how big his town was simply by giving the number of saloons on Main Street.

Sealing a deal with a drink was almost as legal in the eyes of most miners as the most carefully drawn and signed contract.

Miners with good luck drank to celebrate while their less fortunate colleagues drank to drown their sorrows. It doesn't take much to come up with an excuse to lift a drink or two, or three, or four...

In Virginia City, life revolved around its saloons. It is estimated that the consumption rate for whiskey was one quart per person per day.

This Tonopah saloon photo shows a typical barroom scene in the year 1910.
(Nevada Historical Society)

The honky-tonks and gambling dens of Nevada flourished wherever they popped up, and prostitutes and dance hall girls helped draw in the miners to the establishment. Whiskey was generally all sold at the same price, "two bits". The third or fourth one was usually on the house.

Saloon art was as much a part of the saloon environment as was the whiskey. Most of the indigenous art of the boom camps was of the "saloon" variety, and collectors have removed much of it from the state.

Many saloons featured expensive drawings of nubile girls hanging at eye level behind the bar. They were usually totally naked or modestly screened by the use of a small fan or article of clothing, such as a scarf.

Scales weren't necessarily used for smaller transactions. Bartenders, clerks, faro dealers and madams were adept at extracting a pinch or two of dust from a prospector's buckskin gold sack.

There are no records establishing how many pinches a girl could get for her services, but the women-starved miners who outnumbered females 200 to one weren't at all reluctant to pay the price for feminine companionship.

Resources

1. "Desert Challenge," by Richard Lillard
2. "Saloons of Nevada," by Raymond M. Smith

About the Author

Alton Pryor has been a writer for magazines, newspapers, and wire services. He worked for United Press International in their Sacramento Bureau, handling both printed press as well as radio news.

He then worked for the Salinas Californian daily newspaper for five years.

In 1963, he joined California Farmer magazine where he worked as a field editor for 27 years.

When that magazine was sold, the new owners forced him into retirement, which did not suit him at all. He then turned to writing books.

He is a graduate of California State Polytechnic University, San Luis Obispo, where he earned a Bachelor of Science degree in journalism.

Alton Pryor is the author of ten books, seven of which are on California and western history. Pryor is the author of the following books:

- *Little Known Tales in California History*
- *Classic Tales in California History*
- *California's Hidden Gold*
- *Outlaws and Gunslingers*
- *Publish It Yourself*
- *Historic California, It's Colorful Names and How It Got Them*
- *Jonathan's Red Apple Tree*
- *Those Wild and Lusty Gold Camps (out of print)*
- *Little Known Tales in Nevada History*

171

Raymond M. Smith, 167, 192
Reno, 13, 35, 43, 44, 45, 46, 47, 54, 56, 61, 65, 100, 106, 111, 112, 114, 115, 119, 120, 141, 151, 186
Reuel Colt Gridley, 156
Rhyolite, 31, 33, 41
Richard E., 33, 43, 90
Richard Gordon Lillard, 90
Richard Lillard, 192
Richard M. Bucke, 23
Robert G. Dean, 18
Rock Springs, 170
Rube Bryan, 32
Russell R. Elliott, 27, 34, 39, 71, 90, 100, 115, 120, 141, 189
Sacramento, 17, 19, 156, 174, 195
Sacramento Union, 17, 19
Salt Lake City, 98, 111, 131, 174
Samuel Langhorne Clemens, 76
Samuel Morse, 174
Samuel Youngs, 148
San Francisco, 18, 56, 79, 80, 103, 111, 127, 137, 138, 139, 156, 175, 179, 188, 189
San Joaquin *Republican*, 19
Sand Mountain, 106, 107, 109, 110
Sanitary Fund, 156, 157
Sardine Valley House, 58
Sawtooth Mountain, 43
Senator William A. Clark, 99
Sessions S. Wheeler, 65
Seymour, Indiana, 54
Shawn O'Farrell, 190
Sheep Range, 35
Sheriff Charley Pegg, 57
Sheriff Joe Keate, 125
Sheriff Robert Shirley, 45
Shorty Harris, 30, 33
Sierra, 16, 17, 21, 56, 58, 65, 74, 75, 138, 142, 143, 144, 175
Sierra Lake, 17
Sierra Nevada, 17, 21, 138, 142

Sierra Valley, 58
Sierras, 28, 113
Silver City, 62, 64
Sing Sing Prison, 45
Singing Sands, 108
Six Mile Canyon, 178
Six-Mile Canyon, 25, 26, 188
Slavonian Chief, 49
Southern Klondyke, 87, 88
Southern Klondyke Mining District, 87
Sportsman's Hall, 74
St. Joseph, 174, 175
St. Thomas, 125
Standard Mine, 140
State Printing Office, 69
State Route 58, 43
State Telegraph Company, 174
Strawberry, 74
Susanville, 73
Sutro Tunnel, 14, 186, 187, 188
Tasker Oddie, 89
Territorial Enterprise, 12, 18, 19, 28, 73, 74, 76, 77
Territorial Governor James Nye, 148
Texas, 164, 174
The Big Bonanza, 27, 28
The Desert Lake, 65
The Old Spanish Trail, 98
The Sagebrush State, 120
The Silver State, 27, 39, 65, 71, 77, 96, 100
The Story of the Mine, 27
This Was Nevada, 20, 43, 47, 59, 66, 86, 96
Tilton Cockerill, 54, 55
Tonopah, 3, 12, 30, 35, 41, 87, 88, 89, 107, 108, 165, 191
Tonopah & Tidewater, 42
Treasure City, 181, 182, 183, 184
Treasure Hill, 14, 181, 182, 183

Order Form

Stagecoach Publishing
5360 Campcreek Loop
Roseville, CA. 95747
(916) 771-8166
Email: stagecoach@surewest.net
www.stagecoachpublishing.com

Quantity	Price	Total
____California's Hidden Gold	$11.95	_____
____Classic Tales in CA. History	$11.95	_____
____Fascinating Women in California History	$11.95	_____
____Historic California	$ 9.95	_____
____Jonathan's Red Apple Tree	$ 3.95	_____
____Little Known Tales in California History	$11.95	_____
____Publish It Yourself	$ 9.95	_____
____Outlaws and Gunslingers	$ 9.95	_____
____Little Known Tales in Nevada History	$11.95	_____

Date:_____

Credit Card #:_____

Exp. Date:_____Telephone:_____

Name:_____

Address:_____

_____

Signature:_____

175